Advance Praise for

Teaching for Liberation

"*Teaching for Liberation* is a must-read that propels its readers into the urgent work of dreaming into the future of hip-hop education. It sits us at the feet of noted scholars, decades of research, wisdom, and practice to forward the critical power of hip-hop culture and educational justice."
—Jamila Lyiscott, Associate Professor of Social Justice Education Founding Co-director of The Center of Racial Justice and Youth Engaged Research University of Massachusetts Amherst

"As Hip Hop has reached its 50th year, and as the field of Hip Hop Education has further matured, Adjapong and Allen interrogate the most pressing questions facing the field and its praxisioners today. This book is a compilation of wisdom from Hip Hop Education's most influential and forward-thinking sages. Both in form and substance, Adjapong and Allen stretch our imagination for the radical possibilities for the future of Hip Hop Education and education writ-large."
—Daren Graves, Professor of Social Work and Education Simmons University

"In their insightful new book, "Teaching for Liberation," Adjapong and Allen remind us that, first and foremost, hip-hop is a culture of possibility. The history of hip-hop illustrates the magic that happens when we allow youth to be free. By pushing us to re-member the cultural and soulful spirit that formed its roots, the authors compel us to give Black and Latinx youth their long due respect. This book also honors the researchers who have long valued the ingenuity of hip-hop youth and staked careers on documenting that brilliance. In the beautiful tradition of the porch and the stoop, readers are gifted the opportunity to witness rich conversations with hip-hop intellectual trailblazers. In these truth-telling talks, these prolific scholars reflect on how far we have come and use that prideful history to propel us forward in new, life-giving directions."
—Toby Jenkins, Associate Provost & Professor University of South Carolina

"Teaching for Liberation is a powerful journey into our wildest dreams for the future of education and hip-hop. Grounding this exploration in conversations with pivotal scholars and community-engaged educators, Drs. Adjapong and Allen engage readers in a dialogue that honors hip-hop's 50-year history, reflects on where the field of hip-hop education is now and bridges theory and practice providing practical tools to begin working toward a future rooted in empowerment and liberation."

—Courtney Rose, Professor of Education, Public Scholar and Author of Woven Together: How Unpacking Your Teaching Identity Creates a Stronger Learning Community

"Adjapong and Allen's book offers a glimpse into the thinking of prominent scholars and educators who have been critical to the development of the field of Hip Hop Education. If you weren't backstage, or in the teacher's lounge, this book takes you there."

—Casey Philip Wong, Ph.D. Assistant Professor of Social Foundations of Education at Georgia State University

Teaching for Liberation

Hip-Hop Education
Innovation, Inspiration, Elevation

Edmund Adjapong and Chris Emdin
General Editors

Vol. 4

Edmund Adjapong and Kelly Allen

Teaching for Liberation

On Freedom Dreaming in the Field of Hip-Hop Education

Foreword by Yolanda Sealey-Ruiz

PETER LANG
Lausanne • Berlin • Bruxelles • Chennai • New York • Oxford

Library of Congress Cataloging-in-Publication Data

Names: Adjapong, Edmund, author. | Allen, Kelly, author.
Title: Teaching for liberation on freedom dreaming in the field of hip-hop education / Edmund Adjapong, Kelly Allen.
Description: New York, NY: Peter Lang, [2023] | Series: Hip-hop education, 2643-5551; vol 4 | Includes bibliographical references.
Identifiers: LCCN 2023031508 (print) | LCCN 2023031509 (ebook) | ISBN 9781636673691 (paperback) | ISBN 9781636673707 (pdf) | ISBN 9781636673714 (epub)
Subjects: LCSH: Hip-hop based education. | Hip-hop--Influence. | Authors–Interviews. | Educators–Interviews. | Culturally relevant pedagogy.
Classification: LCC LC1099.515.H57 A35 2023 (print) | LCC LC1099.515.H57 (ebook) | DDC 370.117–dc23/eng/20230816
LC record available at https://lccn.loc.gov/2023031508
LC ebook record available at https://lccn.loc.gov/2023031509
DOI 10.3726/b20993

Bibliographic information published by the **Deutsche Nationalbibliothek.**
The German National Library lists this publication in the German National Bibliography; detailed bibliographic data is available on the Internet at http://dnb.d-nb.de.

Cover design by Peter Lang Group AG

ISSN 2643-5551 (print) ISSN 2643-556X (online)
ISBN 9781636673691 (paperback)
ISBN 9781636673707 (ebook)
ISBN 9781636673714 (epub)
DOI 10.3726/b20993

© 2023 Peter Lang Group AG, Lausanne
Published by Peter Lang Publishing Inc., New York, USA
info@peterlang.com—www.peterlang.com
All rights reserved.

All parts of this publication are protected by copyright.
Any utilization outside the strict limits of the copyright law, without the permission of the publisher, is forbidden and liable to prosecution.
This applies in particular to reproductions, translations, microfilming, and storage and processing in electronic retrieval systems.

This publication has been peer reviewed.

CONTENTS

Foreword — vii

Introduction — 1

Chapter 1 Centering Youth Culture in Hip-Hop Education: Keeping it Real with Gloria Ladson-Billings — 11

Chapter 2 Intentional Centering of Hip-Hop within and beyond Educational Spaces: Keeping it Real with P. Thandi Hicks Harper — 23

Chapter 3 Interrogating Anti-Blackness in Relationship to Hip-Hop: Keeping it Real with Ian Levy — 33

Chapter 4 Towards a Critical Centering of Youth Perspectives on Hip-Hop Education: Keeping it Real with David Stovall — 45

Chapter 5 Cultivating Intersectional Perspectives of Hip-Hop Education: Keeping it Real with Marcella Runell Hall — 57

Chapter 6	On Youth-Centered Hip-Hop Pedagogies and Praxis: Keeping it Real with Lauren Kelly	73
Chapter 7	On Authenticity from a Student and Teacher Perspective: Keeping it Real with Victoria Richardson	83
Chapter 8	The Power of Hip-Hop as a Tool: Keeping it Real with Christopher Emdin	93
Chapter 9	Towards Realizing Freedom Dreams: Reflections and Next Steps	107

FOREWORD

The Lineage, Lessons, and Legacy of Hip-Hop: Freedom Dreaming for the Field of Education and Beyond by Yolanda Sealey-Ruiz

Since I am a storyteller and poet, I'd like to begin with a Bronx tale:

> I came of age
> in the South Bronx.
> Other than its fame
> as the birthplace of Hip-Hop,
> my neighborhood was just like other hoods
> in America—
> A poor community rich
> in potential & possibility because of its youth.
> Rap music guided us—
> Grandmaster Flash, a few blocks away,
> Easy A.D. of Cold Crush, a few floors above.
> We were of housing projects & tenement buildings,
> wrapped in the security of our youth.
> We were young.

> We were Black & Boricua.
> We were optimistic.
> We were infinite.
> We dreamed fearlessly
> as our parents made a way
> out of no way.
> It wasn't until we grew up that we realized
> how much the world was against us.[1]

Hip-Hop is undoubtedly one of the most creative, radically imaginative cultural art forms that America has ever seen. It is no exaggeration that its creation and the magnitude of its influence *were dreams* manifested by the youth of my South Bronx community. Hip-Hop was our inspiration to imagine a world that did not yet exist for us: a world where Black and Latinx people were seen in our full humanity; a time and place where our creativity and brilliance led to equal opportunities for us to thrive. Our dreams for a humane existence for ourselves and those in similar communities across the nation pushed us to press on and be courageous in expressing our discontent and outrage at the conditions in which we were forced to live. Belief in our dreams propelled our mental and emotional strength to reimagine our conditions and reshape the broken world that was handed to us as our destiny. Let's pause for a moment and think about the significance of this: the ability of a people to create an art form during moments of degradation and despair and use it for their survival. Brilliant. Some may suggest that the creation of hip-hop is an example of Plato's (1943) inspired "necessity is the mother of invention" phenomenon. Yet others—namely those who were present at hip-hop's birth and came of age in its midst—understand the fearlessness it takes to *create something* when all is crumbling around you. The creation of hip-hop and how the youth of my Bronx community used it to understand the world we were given is nothing short of a miracle. How we used the art form as a method to navigate violence and uncertainty and leave an indelible mark on the world in the process is the direct result of our audacity to dream.

---

1 This poem, titled "Lolo Jones," will appear in a poetic memoir that Yolanda is currently writing.

Hip-Hop and the Quest for Freedom Dreaming

Our deepest desire was to be free. We dreamed of a world different from the one that was thrust upon us. We desired and deserved an existence void of excessive poverty, racism, drug epidemics, and discrimination from a government that created policies resulting in inferior education, lack of job opportunities, and constant attacks on our humanity. Individuals, like myself, who grew up in The South Bronx during the early decades of hip-hop knew we were all trapped in a cycle of struggle. The five elements of hip-hop culture were our "blackprint" (Bertrand & Porcher, 2020); those elements represented our voice of resistance, the will to survive, and the courage to use our radical visions to create a world we were worthy of inhabiting. The Black and Latino youth who created hip-hop had dreams of freedom. In *Freedom Dreams*, Robin D. G. Kelley (2002) wrote about the dreams his mother had for her family, even as they lived in their impoverished Harlem/Washington Heights apartment building:

> So with her eyes wide open my mother dreamed and dreamed some more, describing what life could be for us. She wasn't talking about some postmortem world, some kind of heaven or afterlife; and she was not speaking of reincarnation (which she believes in by the way). She dreamed of land, a spacious house, fresh air, organic food, and endless meadows without boundaries, free of evil and violence, free of toxins and environmental hazards, free of poverty, racism, sexism…just free. She never talked about how we might create such a world, nor connected her vision to any political ideology. But she convinced my siblings and me that change is possible and that we didn't have to be stuck there forever. (p. 2)

Kelley and I grew up in similar neighborhood conditions. I pay homage to the dreams and resilience of the youth in my community in the poem "The Bronx, circa 1982," which speaks to a very specific decade in Bronx history when white landlords burned down their properties—the buildings that we lived in—to receive insurance checks and flee our predominantly Black and Latinx neighborhoods. In the poem, I express how The Bronx helped to shape me into the woman I am today, and how much I am in awe of our commitment to our survival in the face of extreme challenges, such as having our homes burned down and being displaced while those in power simply stood by and watched.

"The Bronx, circa 1982"

I am always thinking of that place/
the hood that nurtured me & helped
to shape me into the woman/
I am...& becoming.
I have always held you
close/
wrapped in my arms
of blazing fire & ashes/
I knew you before you knew
yourself/
I saved you when others
wanted to throw you/
back to the ashes
from which you rose/
like a Phoenix you came
rising & rushing/
toward the midnight sky.[2]

Dreaming takes courage and fortitude; it takes commitment and strength in the face of adversity. Hip-Hop and the youth who created it endured to leave a legacy for today's educators to learn from and bring to their classrooms in ways that honor the struggles and accomplishments of the youth and the conditions propelling them to dream. As the nation celebrates the 50th Anniversary of hip-hop in 2023, people in Black and Latinx communities are still dreaming as we face the reality that a world built on anti-blackness is ever-present. The dubious truth for the Black and Latinx youth who created this culture is that while they are constantly discredited and shunned for who they are as a people, the culture they created sells everything from clothing to cars. The power of our culture is consumed and celebrated even as we continue to face unequal opportunities, police brutality, unfair treatment in schools, and inferior education.

---

2 "The Bronx, circa 1982" first appeared in *Love from the Vortex & Other Poems* by Yolanda Sealey-Ruiz.

Hip-Hop Past, Present, and a Pass to the Future

Over the course of the last 50 years, hip-hop has evolved from a local art form centered on the five elements of rapping, DJ-ing, break dancing, graffiti art, and self-knowledge to a global cultural movement. As this volume emphasizes, it is critical to have an eye on the future of hip-hop's influence, particularly in education, but it is perhaps just as significant to glance over its formidable past. In 1973, hip-hop was born as a product of social action in the Bronx River Projects in the South Bronx. Afrika Bambaataa, a former 'War Lord' of the street gang the Spades and leader of the Zulu Nation organization, is recognized as the father of hip-hop consciousness. In an effort to end the gang violence that plagued the South Bronx at the time, Bambaataa, along with the technical genius of DJ Kool Herc, organized large block parties where young people came to channel the tensions of the street through dancing and socializing in a safe and positive environment (Chang, 2005). Rap, as an art form, began as a personal narrative, telling the individual stories of urban lives ignored by the mainstream media. In the late 1970s, hip-hop took the main stage both as a cultural phenomenon and a commercial success (Rose, 1994, pp. 2). Throughout the 1980s and 1990s, hip-hop became solidified as a culture that involved its five elements while remaining true to its roots in the Black Power and Civil Rights movements (Collins, 2006). Hip-Hop's participation in and shaping of the larger American culture provides a vehicle for BIPOC youth, and Black youth in particular, to resist the status quo of disempowerment that has been prescribed for them. Early on, Rose (1994) argued that "Hip-Hop is a cultural form that attempts to negotiate the experiences of marginalization, brutality, truncated opportunity, and oppression with the cultural imperatives of African American and Caribbean history, identity, and community" (p. 21). Decades of historical and empirical research, including this present volume, confirm the indisputable influence of hip-hop culture on student learning (Adjapong, 2017; Bynoe, 2004; Chang, 2005; Dyson, 2007; Emdin, 2010; Forman & Neal, 2004; Ginwright, 2004; Hicks Harper, 2006; Hill, 2009; Kelly, 2013; Love, 2013; Petchauer, 2007; Rose, 1994; Siedel, 2011; Yasin, 2014; Runell & Diaz, 2007).

This book, *Teaching for Liberation: Radically Dreaming about the Future of Hip-Hop Education* should be on the bookshelves of every teacher and scholar—whether they identify and participate in the field of hip-hop education or not.

It is a tour-de-force showing the possibility, power, and promise of a pedagogy that bears the ethos of creativity, inclusion, and belonging. This volume captures and beautifully articulates ideas for educators to radicalize the stale, culturally irrelevant, status-quo education centered on testing that brings misery to both teachers and students. Hip-Hop education enlivens the school experience for teachers and students; it is a portal of possibility that allows teachers and students to see each other and learn from each other's lives while engaging in a history and approach to education that is life-giving and joyful. As Dr. Adjapong said in his dialogue with Dr. Allen in the introduction of this book, "We want to be authentic to hip-hop culture. This means situating hip-hop's origin story, and why understanding how hip-hop came to be, and the context in which hip-hop was birthed. Further, understanding how hip-hop exists within communities of color in very powerful, and liberatory ways."

Drs. Adjapong and Allen have written themselves into this lineage of hip-hop education and extended the important conversation about its connection to culturally relevant teaching. Indeed, hip-hop Education, as Dr. Gloria Ladson-Billings (2018) referred to it, is a "pedagogy of opposition" (p. xx of this volume); it is also a pedagogy of refusal and resistance to the status quo of educational practices in schools. The genesis of hip-hop was opposing, refusing, and resisting the degradation and inequality created for and experienced by Black and Latinx communities. Drs. Adjapong and Allen's original research and deft analysis of those they interviewed provide a clear vision of the essence of hip-hop and how it must show up in classrooms. As they reflect on the powerful past of hip-hop and its influence on education, they also provide a forward-thinking approach to correct ways that hip-hop education has been misapplied in classrooms and stake a claim for its future. In truth, there have been hit-and-miss results when implementing hip-hop in education. Those educators who approach the pedagogy from a surface level and think it is merely about getting kids to write rhymes and tap syncopated beats on their desks have missed its point and power entirely. Hip-Hop education requires full heart, open mind, and a deep respect for the history of the culture and those who created it and maintain it today. Drs. Adjapong and Allen asserted in their introduction: "We also intended this text to be used as an opportunity to radically dream and imagine where we want the field of hip-hop and education to go." The book draws on several decades of research on hip-hop and its significance to the field of education, and these chapters present readers with an innovative take on hip-hop education through engaging conversations with noted scholars and practitioners as well as pointed analyses.

Hip-Hop's original goal was liberation. The cultural art form was born of youth dreams in the early 1970s, and this remains true to this goal today. As Dr. Adjapong noted in the introduction, "It's important to recognize that hip-hop was created to liberate and provide opportunities for youth and historically marginalized communities to gather, engage, and celebrate their communities." Educators must implement hip-hop pedagogy in a way that honors the legacy of the cultural art form. The youth in my Bronx neighborhood and other youth in similar communities had big dreams, and hip-hop became the voice of those dreams. Children in classrooms are still dreaming, but the important questions are: Are educators making space to hear those dreams? Do students have the freedom to claim the genius that already lies within? Are they allowed to be like my childhood friend Oscar and dream of a world that is possible for those who dare?

> Excerpt from "Oscar the Dreamer"
>
> We were our parents' wildest dreams
> when they boarded planes from
> Puerto Rico & Barbados; taking the train
> from a segregated South that wanted them
> to emigrate brokenness & sadness, but they resisted
> & birthed us, the promise & possibility of all
> that was joyful—
> All that was now harvesting
> on makeshift fields, in underfunded classrooms,
> public housing & apartments filled with
> love
>   laughter
>   & the hope
> for us to become all that we could be
> and everything WE ARE.[3]

References

Adjapong, E. S. (2017). Bridging theory and practice in the urban science classroom: A framework for hip-hop pedagogy in STEM. *Critical Education*, 8(15), 5–22.

Bertrand, S., & Porcher, K. (2020). The Black Gaze Podcast. *Paine artistry*. https://podcasts.apple.com/us/podcast/black-gaze/id1512508384

---

3 This poem, titled "Oscar the Dreamer," will appear in a poetic memoir that Yolanda is currently writing.

Bynoe, Y. (2004). *Stand and deliver: Political activism, leadership, and hip-hop culture.* Soft Skull Press.

Chang, J. (2005). *Can't stop, won't stop: A history of the hip-hop generation.* St. Martin's Press.

Collins, P. H. (2006). *From Black power to hip-hop: Racism, nationalism, and feminism.* Temple University Press.

Dyson, M. E. (2007). *Know what I mean: Reflections on hip-hop.* Basic Civitas Books.

Emdin, C. (2010). *Urban science education for the hip hop generation.* Sense Publishers.

Forman, M., & Neal, M. A. (Eds.). (2004). *That's the joint! The hip-hop studies reader* (1st ed.). Routledge. https://doi.org/10.4324/9780203642191.

Ginwright, S. (2004). *Black in school: Afrocentric reform, urban youth and the promise of hip-hop culture.* Teachers College Press.

Hicks Harper, P. T. (2006). *Hip-Hop development: Exploring hip-hop culture as a youth engagement tool for successful community building.* bILLO Communications and the Youth Popular Culture Institute.

Hill, M. L. (2009). *Beats, rhymes and classroom life: Hip-Hop pedagogy and the politics of identity.* Teachers College Press.

Jowett, B. (1943). *Plato's the republic.* Book, Inc.

Kelley, R. D. G. (2002). *Freedom dreams: The Black radical imagination.* Beacon Press.

Kelly, L. L. (2013). Hip-Hop literature: The politics, poetics, and power of hip-hop in the English classroom. *English Journal, 102*(5), 50–55. https://www.jstor.org/stable/24484092

Ladson-Billings, G. (2018). From big homie the OG, to GLB: Hip-Hop and the reinvention of a pedagogue. In C. Emdin & E. Adjapong (Eds.), *#HipHopEd: The compilation on hip-hop education* (pp. 21–26). Brill.

Love, B. L. (2013). *Hip-Hop's Li'l Sistas speak: Negotiating hip-hop identities and politics in the new South.* Peter Lang.

Petchauer, E. M. (2007). *"Welcome to the underground": Portraits of worldview and education among hip-hop collegians.* Unpublished doctoral dissertation, Regent University, Virginia Beach, VA.

Rose, T. (1994). *Black noise: Rap music and Black culture in contemporary America.* Hanover: University Press of New England.

Runell, M., & Diaz, M. (2007). *The hip-hop education guidebook, Volume 1.* Lulu.com.

Sealey-Ruiz, Y. (2020). *Love from the vortex & other poems.* Kaleidoscope Vibrations.

Siedel, S. (2011). *Hip-Hop genius: Remixing high school education.* R&L Education.

Yasin, J. (2014). Hip-Hop culture as a tool in the teaching-learning process. In K. Lomotey (Ed.), *The handbook of urban education* (pp. 413–430). Routledge.

INTRODUCTION

On Freedom Dreaming in the Field of Hip-Hop Education

Edmund: What's the premise of the book?

Kelly: Hip-Hop and freedom dreaming.

Edmund: The goal of this book is to recognize and acknowledge all the work, research, and literature that has been produced in the field of hip-hop and education. We also intended this text to be used as an opportunity to radically dream and imagine where we want the field of hip-hop and education to go. I think at this point we recognize that there have been a lot of scholars and practitioners who have leveraged hip-hop within educational spaces in an effective manner, and this text is meant to pay homage to those folks. We also wanted to create an opportunity for folks who have contributed to the field of hip-hop and education to reflect on the field and offer a path forward. We also want to radically dream as a community about the direction and intention of the field, particularly in recognizing that hip-hop is celebrating its 50th anniversary this year (2023) and has existed as a culture that society didn't really imagine making it this far.

Kelly: I think a lot of us who contribute to the field of hip-hop in education recognize that there's so much more potential that hip-hop and education can offer.

Like, we haven't arrived at the destination yet?

There is great work happening in many spaces, but there could be more intentional and comprehensive approaches to the use of hip-hop in educational spaces and that's the need to start freedom dreaming.

Edmund: Yeah, and this book is a push for that.

This book is a push for us to be intentional and deliberate about how we imagine hip-hop to exist within educational spaces. This book also offers an opportunity to critique how hip-hop has existed within educational spaces thus far and to provide possibilities for practitioners, scholars, and researchers to consider how they want to engage in hip-hop and education in different ways.

Ultimately, you know, we want to keep it real with the field [of hip-hop and education] right?

We want to keep it real around where the field has been and what has been offered in relation to the use of hip-hop in educational spaces because we can also argue that some of the offerings have not necessarily been authentic to hip-hop culture right? Some of the offerings that have been pawned off as hip-hop in education mainly reflect the commercialized aspect of hip-hop.

We want to be authentic to hip-hop culture. This means situating hip-hop's origin story, and why understanding how hip-hop came to be and the context in which hip-hop was birthed. Further, understanding how hip-hop exists within communities of color in very powerful, and liberatory ways.

It's important to recognize that hip-hop was created to liberate and provide opportunities for youth and historically marginalized communities to gather, engage, and celebrate their communities.

Our goal and objective for leveraging hip-hop in educational spaces are to provide these same opportunities that hip-hop was originally created for to exist within schools and educational spaces.

Kelly: There's so much more work to do, and we haven't arrived.

And if we embark on this goal of freedom dreaming in this book without keeping it real in the process, we're just going to be pushing this idea of hip-hop in education that is going to end up replicating the same oppressive, marginalizing systems that we, and hip-hop as a culture, is looking to disrupt. And so at the core of this book, it's this whole idea that as we continue this work, we have to keep it real with ourselves, with the culture, with our students, and with our community.

'cause that's really the question at the end of the day
[pause]

What is going to help us realize this goal of liberatory education?

Conversations on Keeping It Real

This book is composed of *conversations on keeping real* with scholars, educators, and community members who have contributed to and have engaged in research in the field of hip-hop and education. *Keeping it real* is a hip-hop credo that has existed since the inception of hip-hop and continues to exist as a cultural code and badge of cultural authenticity to this day (Basu, 1998). Keeping it real as it relates to hip-hop means having a deep understanding and knowledge of the culture and history of hip-hop as a means of invoking authenticity within hip-hop (Williams, 2007). Keeping it real considers the authenticity of hip-hop as it relates to the origins of hip-hop culture and the context in which hip-hop was created. Hip-Hop is a culture that was created organically by Black, Latinx, and immigrant communities in the Bronx during a socio-economic crisis during the 1970s. The birth of hip-hop was a response to the social injustices that Black and immigrant communities faced while living in urban centers during the socio-economic crisis of the 1970s. Hip-Hop was created as a result of the blatant disregard for Black and Brown lives and served as a social and therapeutic outlet (Emdin et al., 2016) for Black and Latinx youth, many of whom were either immigrants or first-generation Americans, in response to the effects of industrialization in the Bronx, including the Cross-Bronx Expressway (Chang, 2007; Rose, 1994). To this day, hip-hop continues to be innovated by Black and brown youth, particularly within urban centers.

The Cross-Bronx Expressway is a highway that spans 7 miles and connects the I-95 northeastern corridor through New York City. Robert Moses, an urban developer, and his supporters decided to build the Cross-Bronx Expressway and as a result, displaced more than 1,500 families in the Bronx. This led to the destruction of homes, and communities within a predominantly Black community causing immense grief for displaced residents. Moses insisted on the development of the Cross-Bronx Expressway through a predominantly Black community although he could have built the expressway along another route that would have displaced far fewer residents and cost much less money (Ploschnitzki, 2017). Hip-Hop emerged as an art form as a way to cope, find joy, and celebrate community in the midst of the industrialization of the Bronx and social-economic turmoil. Further, hip-hop was used as a platform to share the perspectives and experiences of historically marginalized groups with the world. The power of music and camaraderie united Bronx youth during the 1970s and continues to unite the global hip-hop community today. Hip-Hop culture continues to be used as a tool to promote social justice and advocate for the needs of historically marginalized communities and provides opportunities for young people, adults, and elders to gather, dance, and ultimately enjoy life regardless of the harsh realities they face.

Hip-Hop has undoubtedly influenced American culture. As hip-hop has gained popularity within American society, it has also been co-opted by mainstream society. We argue that the commercial viability of hip-hop aesthetics and sensibilities can lead to the destruction and exploitation of hip-hop culture and has allowed outsiders of hip-hop culture to benefit monetarily. Hip-Hop, like other Black musical genres, has been a huge source of profit for America's recording industry. According to ABC News, the hip-hop market grew to nearly 16 billion dollars by 2016. Hip-Hop, like any culture or art form that has gained mainstream notoriety globally, has fallen victim to the negative effects of capitalism, which has pushed it away from its origins anchored in social justice. The recording industry is aware of the profitability of hip-hop by marketing directly toward White teens, who account for the top consumer of hip-hop music and artifacts. The recording industry takes advantage of this notion by continuing to promote and commercialize negative tropes and narratives of Blackness to hip-hop's top consumers—White teens. Major record labels primarily promote hip-hop artists who perpetuate negative stereotypes of Blackness for White teen consumption, which further contributes to society's negative perception of hip-hop culture, and in turn, Black communities who create and innovate the culture. In her critique of the commercialization of rap music, Blair posits, "there is something horribly wrong with a dominant community repeatedly co-opting the cultural forms of oppressed communities, stripping them of their vitality and form, the heritage of their creators, and then popularizing them" (Blair, 2004, p. 21). White youth who are the top consumers of hip-hop music co-opt cultural forms of Black and Brown communities and are often celebrated for replicating stereotypical tropes of these communities for their entertainment, popularity, and social media exposure. For example, a young White woman named Brook went viral on TikTok for rapping the lyrics to a song titled *Took Her to the O* by the late rapper King Von during a wedding reception. King Von was a Drill (rapper) artist whose music is often criticized for focusing on crime and the daily ordeals of life on the streets. The song *Took Her to the O* is a song about King Von engaging in violent behavior with a woman's boyfriend and subsequently taking the woman back to his neighborhood, "the O." Brook's video of her rapping along to King Von's *Took Her to the O* went viral with commentators remarking and amazed by a white woman being able to recall and recite lyrics to a popular Drill song. The video of Brook became a viral sensation because it is not an everyday site where you see a stereotypical "innocent" white woman reciting Drill song lyrics which are often criticized for focusing on the crime and the daily ordeals of life on the streets in Black and Brown communities. The reality is that Drill music and artists have been under attack by politicians and law enforcement which demonstrates harsh implications for the Black and Brown artists, but a white woman is glorified and celebrated for reciting the same lyrics (Vozick-Levinson, 2022). This video going viral contributes to the notion of commercialized hip-hop as a white woman was able to leverage hip-hop culture to create a social media career while Black and Brown people are criticized for creating and consuming this same music. For white consumers, drill music and hip-hop, more broadly, is often positioned as entertainment. For others, hip-hop is a culture that is aligned with lived experiences, values, and simply a way of life. The inequitable treatment of Black artists and white consumers is a manifestation of anti-Blackness and systemic racism. While commercialized hip-hop doubles down on tropes of Blackness, it's important that we recognize that hip-hop continues to exist and is innovated within local communities that provide authentic and critical accounts of the Black experience and reality.

Our articulation of *keeping it real* in hip-hop encourages participants of hip-hop culture and those who engage in hip-hop education to consider the origins of hip-hop, which are anchored in social justice for the benefit of Black and historically marginalized communities. This consideration ensures that hip-hop is constantly used as a tool to address inequities that individuals and communities experience and can counter the commercialized realities of hip-hop culture. Similar to the challenges of hip-hop in mainstream culture as it relates to capitalism, these challenges also exist within educational spaces. If educators who are utilizing a commercialized perception of hip-hop to incorporate into educational spaces, they may be in danger of replicating the same consumer understanding of hip-hop. If educators take a commercialized view of hip-hop into the classroom, they position their students as entities to be entertained, not to address social injustices that persist in their communities. Therefore, hip-hop will be leveraged to "hook" students into learning through superficial implementations of hip-hop instead of being implemented to disrupt the inequitable teaching and learning systems in school, which is the primary aim of hip-hop education. Hip-Hop within educational spaces should be used to benefit students and gain a deeper understanding of marginalized communities instead of using hip-hop to align students to systems that center and value whiteness. Therefore, we contend that hip-hop educators have to keep it real—and refer to the origins of hip-hop. We have to reject the implementation of hip-hop in schools that seeks to simply hook students into learning. While student engagement is a by-product of implementing hip-hop in educational spaces, it should not be the primary goal. The implementation of hip-hop in schools to simply engage students is a perpetuation of white norms and values that seek to control and silence Black bodies. Instead, keeping it real in the implementation of hip-hop in educational spaces authentically brings hip-hop into schooling spaces to disrupt whitewashed curriculum, invigorate stale pedagogical practices that do not speak to the communicative pathways of Black and Brown students, and encourage youth to identify solutions to challenges that persist in their communities.

Freedom Dreaming a Future for Hip-Hop Education

As hip-hop culture continues to gain popularity, so do the academic examinations of hip-hop culture. Scholars and practitioners have utilized various terminologies in the work they are engaging in around hip-hop within educational spaces such as: *hip-hop based education, hip-hop education, critical hip-hop pedagogy,* and *hip-hop pedagogy.* The aforementioned terms are some of the most prevalent terms that emerge in the literature focused on the use of hip-hop within educational spaces. Hip-Hop based education and hip-hop education are often positioned as different perspectives on the *field* of hip-hop and education as a whole, whereas critical hip-hop pedagogy and hip-hop pedagogy are *frameworks* that seek to actualize the pedagogical implementation of hip-hop in educational spaces. For the purpose of this book, we conceptualize our work through the lens of hip-hop education.

> Hip-Hop education is the field of study that supports scholarship and practice that promotes the use of hip-hop culture and sensibilities across all educational spaces.

Central to our understanding of hip-hop education is the recognition and understanding of the layers of oppression that exist in society and the belief that the many sociocultural identities of students, teachers, and community members matter (Runell & Diaz, 2007). This understanding of oppression and how it manifests in our society recognizes that schooling structures as they currently exist are oppressive to systematically marginalized groups and must be reimagined. In the process of reimagining, Emdin (2018) argues that a core component of realizing hip-hop education in schools is understanding that "everything that happens within schools as it relates to the education of youth from the hip-hop generation and beyond must be changed" (p. 3).

In the process of change, or transformation, that Emdin (2018) discusses, there must be room for envisioning the future of education. While it is necessary to acknowledge and address the challenges that persist within education, it is also important to envision what the future of education could be and how educational systems can be increasingly inclusive and support the liberation of systematically marginalized groups. We cannot solely focus on the problems that exist in education, but we must allow ourselves the freedom to dream of a future of education that doesn't perpetuate systemic oppression.

In his book, *Freedom Dreams: The Black Radical Imagination*, Robin D.G. Kelley shares,

> "without new visions, we don't know what to build, only what to knock down. We not only end up confused, rudderless, and cynical, but we forget that making a revolution is not a series of clever maneuvers and tactics but a process that can and must transform us" (p. xii).

While it is imperative to name and dismantle the processes and systems that oppress us, we must also engage in the radical act of freedom dreaming. Freedom dreams not only provide us with a pathway to critically understand and analyze present oppression within educational spaces, but it also provides a radical space to dream about what education without oppression could look like.

In this book, we engage in the act of freedom dreaming as conceptualized by Kelley (2002). We conceptualized this book as a space of radical possibility where we could freedom dream about the future of the field of hip-hop education. Rooted in this radical space, however, is an unapologetic naming and rejection of the oppressive structures and practices that continue to halt the attainment of liberatory education. In this text, we dialogue with scholars in the field of hip-hop education about their personal connections with hip-hop and education, their perceptions of the field, and their freedom dreams for the field of hip-hop education.

The book opens with a conversation with Dr. Gloria Ladson-Billings, who considers the need for educators and scholars to center youth and to position themselves as continual learners in work around hip-hop education. The second chapter articulates tensions between hip-hop education and the norms and expectations of academia while advocating for a focus on youth development in hip-hop through the perspective of Dr. Thandi Hicks Harper. The third chapter highlights a conversation with Dr. Ian Levy, who talks about the influence of whiteness in hip-hop and how pervasive embodiments of anti-Blackness manifest in the way hip-hop education is enacted. The fourth chapter illuminates misappropriations of hip-hop education and drives home the need for educators and scholars engaging in the work to examine their positionality through a conversation with Dr. David Stovall. Then, chapter five spotlights Dr. Marcella Runell Hall who contends that individuals must critically examine how they are embodying hip-hop education in a way that disrupts anti-Blackness, misogyny, and patriarchy. Chapter six features a conversation with Dr. Lauren Kelly, who synthesizes the need for youth centered approaches to hip-hop education and advocates for individuals to trust youth to lead hip-hop engaged work. Chapter seven illuminates student-centered perspectives on hip-hop education and emphasizes the need for authenticity in the work through a discussion with Victoria Richardson. The last conversation, featured in chapter 8, highlights the perspective of Dr. Christopher Emdin who discusses critical hip-hop engaged scholarship and pushes back against the perception that hip-hop education needs to be validated through empirical research methods. The book closes with an outro that synthesizes major takeaways for readers.

Our hope is that the dialogues within this book inspire scholars, educators, and community members and re-energize the field to produce more scholarship and practical applications for the critical implementation of hip-hop within educational spaces so that we can one day actualize our freedom dreams.

References

Basu, D. (1998). What is real about keeping it real? *Postcolonial Studies: Culture, Politics, Economy, 1*(3), 371-387.

Blair, M. E. (2004). Commercialization of the rap music youth subculture.. In M. Neal & M. Forman (Eds.), *That's the Joint* (pp. 497 - 499). Routledge.

Chang, J. (2007). *Can't stop won't stop: A history of the hip hop generation.* St. Martin's Press.

Emdin, C. (2016). *For White folks who teach in the hood… and the rest of y'all too: Reality pedagogy and urban education.* Beacon Press.

Emdin, C. (2018). Introduction. In C. Emdin & E. Adjapong (Eds.), *#HipHopEd: The compilation on hip-hop education, volume 1: Hip hop as education, philosophy, and practice*. Brill Sense.

Hill, M. L. (2009). Bringing back sweet (and not so sweet) memories: The cultural politics of memory, hip hop, and generational identities. *International Journal of Qualitative Studies in Education (QSE), 22*(4), 355–377. https://doi.org/10.1080/09518390902740589.

Kelley, R. (2002). *Freedom dreams: The black radical imagination*. Beacon Press.

Ploschnitzki, P. (2017). *Robert Moses, the construction of the cross Bronx expressway and its impact on the Bronx*. University of Arizona. December 11, 2017. https://www.academia.edu/8799288/_Robert_Moses_the_construction_of_the_Cross-Bronx_Expressway_and_its_impact_on_the_Bronx_

Rose, T. (1994). *Black noise: Rap music and Black culture in contemporary America*. Wesleyan University Press.

Runell, M., & Diaz, M. (2007). *The hip hop education guidebook: Volume 1*. The Hip-Hop Association, Inc.

Williams, J. D. "Tha Realness": In search of hip-hop authenticity. December 14, 2007. CUREJ: College Undergraduate Research Electronic Journal, University of Pennsylvania, https://repository.upenn.edu/curej/78.

Vozick-Levinson, S. (2022). *New York City mayor Eric Adams declares war on Drill Rap*. Rolling Stone. Retrieved July 11, 2022, from https://www.rollingstone.com/music/music-news/mayor-eric-adams-drill-rap-1299108/

· 1 ·

CENTERING YOUTH CULTURE IN HIP-HOP EDUCATION: KEEPING IT REAL WITH GLORIA LADSON-BILLINGS

Dr. Gloria Ladson-Billings is a notable pedagogical theorist, teacher educator, and the former Kellner Family Distinguished Professor of Urban Education in the Department of Educational Policy Studies at the University of Wisconsin, Madison. Many of us refer to Dr. Ladson-Billings as an OG (someone that is an original or originator and especially one who is highly respected or regarded) within the field of hip-hop education and education writ large. Dr. Ladson-Billings is well known for her framework for culturally relevant pedagogy and work in critical race theory.

Edmund: Can you explain how you identify yourself as a scholar?
Dr. Ladson-Billings: So, I'm not sure I totally identify as a scholar? I see myself as a person with an enduring question, and that question is how can we ensure that African American students and other students who are marginalized get quality education? That's the question for me. That's the question for me, both in the academy and beyond the academy.

Dr. Ladson-Billings' positioning of herself as someone with an enduring question is evidenced in the breadth of research she has published and contributed to the field through various mediums focused on African American and other historically oppressed groups. Beyond her work with critical race theory and culturally relevant pedagogy, she has also published extensively on the experiences and perspectives of African American educators and has contributed to thinking about the achievement debt incurred by African American students. Dr. Ladson-Billings' framework for culturally responsive pedagogy laid the foundation for the field of hip-hop and education by highlighting the necessity for the inclusion of youth cultures, values, and identities within both the curriculum and instruction of the classroom. Ladson-Billings (1995a) originally described culturally relevant pedagogy as a "pedagogy of opposition" that was committed to collective empowerment (p. 160). More specifically, Dr. Ladson-Billings (1995a) positions culturally relevant pedagogy as "a pedagogy that empowers students intellectually, socially, emotionally, and politically by using cultural references to impart knowledge, skills, and attitudes" (p.18). Ladson-Billings (1995a) identified culturally relevant pedagogy as an effective way of educating African American students, which rests on the following criteria: "(a) students must experience academic success; (b) students must develop and/or maintain cultural competence, and (c) students must develop a critical consciousness through which they challenge the status quo of the current social order" (p. 160).

Edmund: How do you align yourself with hip-hop in your scholarship, your practice, and your work in general?

Dr. Ladson-Billings: I probably come at hip-hop through the "backdoor," if you will. I'm very interested in youth and youth culture, and because hip-hop so dominates youth culture, there's sort of no way to avoid being involved in it. I'm on the advisory board for the University of Wisconsin, Madison's first-wave, hip-hop art scholars program. I was a faculty member on their advisory board. I thought this was another advisory board. I'll kind of just sit on the side here, I'll chime in at the meetings, but the students came to me deeply concerned about the lack of sort of relevant education courses around hip-hop. And they were like, no, we need you to teach the course. So, I relented. I organized the course. Fortunately, there was a little bit of money attached to it. So it's what allowed me to bring in all kinds of folks. That's really how I got Chris Emdin there, who is someone who can both talk to my students and can talk to the broader public. We had all kinds of folks participate, from Ebro Darden to Davy D. So, the more time I spent working with young people around these issues, the more I learned. And the more I learned, the more I understood what was missing in my own scholarship. I've just completed a third edition of the Dreamkeepers book, and it

> does speak to some of the secondary teachers that I've encountered along the way. One of the things that I felt is missing in Dreamkeepers is that because I work with elementary students, I didn't capture the whole youth culture piece of it. And that's not to suggest that younger students don't consume youth culture. They do. But they don't normally produce it. It has taken me to see that the work that people are doing with youth is an important aspect of this whole thing that I've called culturally relevant pedagogy that the culture is beyond just W.E.B DuBois and Black history. It is what young people are producing.

What is so impactful about Dr. Ladson-Billings' alignment with hip-hop is her willingness to decenter herself in her practice and research. Dr. Ladson-Billings sat on the advisory board for a hip-hop scholar arts program but did not consider her role a central one. While she acknowledged the importance of hip-hop as an aspect of youth culture, it wasn't until her students came to her and encouraged her to become more deeply involved in hip-hop courses on campus that she became more centrally involved. Even when she was tasked with leading the hip-hop course, she positioned herself as a facilitator. As someone who considered herself relatively new to hip-hop at the time, she opted to bring in individuals who could speak to the lived experiences of her students and hip-hop.

It's important to recognize that Dr. Ladson-Billings' is a notable expert in urban education and has extensively studied teaching and learning as it relates to Black teachers and students, but still understands that she is not an expert when it comes to hip-hop culture. Dr. Ladson-Billings' positions herself as a student of the culture while providing opportunities for hip-hop experts to enter her academic space to teach her and her students. Further, Dr. Ladson-Billings' willingness to critique her own research and perspective is important to note. Because her research focused on elementary students, Dr. Ladson-Billings acknowledges that she didn't necessarily consider youth culture as a central piece of her research until she spent more time with students and saw the impact of hip-hop on their lived experiences. This willingness to critique her perspective has expanded her understanding of culturally relevant pedagogy as well as the potential and power of hip-hop, and Dr. Ladson-Billings hopes other educators and researchers can embody this same mindset. Despite the apparent popularity of culturally relevant pedagogy and its wide acceptance, Dr. Ladson-Billings describes her dissatisfaction with many scholars' interpretation of what it means to be culturally relevant (Ladson-Billings, 2014). Dr. Ladson-Billings (2014) argues that many scholars are stuck in superficial and limited notions of culture, and as a result, the fluidity of cultural groups has been regularly lost in the implementation of culturally relevant pedagogy.

> "Today, researchers and practitioners are moving and evolving in new ways that require us to embrace a more dynamic view of culture. As an educational anthropologist, I understand culture as an amalgamation of human activity, production, thought, and belief systems. Typically, we ascribe notions of culture to people who are a part of a nation-state, an ethnic group, or a religious group. Often, we are less definitive about conceptions such as "youth culture" because they are not easily bound by agreed-on or recognizable categories. But, like other cultural groups, youth do maintain notions of membership (i.e., in-group versus out-group), language, art, beliefs, and so on… However, in reality, culture is always changing." (p.75)

Researchers and educators must embrace the fluidity and complexities of youth culture, so they can move towards ways of learning and understanding youth and their culture to shift educational experiences to be more culturally relevant. Dr. Ladson-Billings notes that openness about cultural shifts and a willingness to embrace changes in mindsets and practices is needed to propel education forward.

Kelly: One of my questions, as I'm listening to you talk, is what inspires you to go and explore hip-hop even more? Why is that important for you as you're looking to extend your work?

Dr. Ladson-Billings: I think anybody who calls themselves a scholar or, or a teacher is always a learner. The moment you think you finished learning, you need to get out of this game.

Dr. Ladson-Billings believes that educators and scholars must identify as lifelong learners to be effective in their craft. However, she contends that it is important to set an intention behind your learning even as an educator. This idea reminds us of the philosophy of "Becoming" theorized by Dr. Maxine Greene. Dr. Maxine Greene discusses her philosophy of "Becoming" where she posits,

> "to learn, I believe, is to become, to become different. It is to continue making new connections in experience, new meanings if you like. Meanings are funded, we are told, and offer continually expanding perspectives on the experience. But that depends a good deal on a willingness to go beyond what is--to reach beyond mere facts to widening cognitive or intellectual possibilities" (Greene, 2007).

Maxine Greene shares that learning creates shifts in individuals as new understandings are connected to life experiences. It is ultimately the decision of the scholar or educator to explore and make meaning of new understandings and experiences, which requires challenging our perspectives and understanding of the world. Being a hip-hop educator and scholar requires the decentering of oneself, but also practicing humility in the sense that you may not know or understand a particular phenomenon, but it doesn't mean that the phenomenon cannot be explored and interrogated. Further, not being able to initially understand a phenomenon in relationship to hip-hop does not mean that the phenomenon does not exist. For example, when we identify hip-hop as a culture, understandably there are outsiders of the culture who are ignorant to the customs, norms, shared values, ways of engagement etc. of hip-hop. There are phenomena that exist within hip-hop that only folks who identify as part of hip-hop can understand. If you do not understand something, it is impossible to adequately interrogate it. Hence, the importance of decentering oneself and *positioning oneself as a student of hip-hop* is necessary for those who identify as hip-hop educators and those who are curious as to how hip-hop can be leveraged within educational spaces as hip-hop is a rapid and ever-changing culture that exists differently in various settings.

Edmund:	What are your thoughts on the field of hip-hop and education right now? What inspires you about what's going on in the field right now?
Dr. Ladson-Billings:	Well, I'm of two minds because there are always those folks who jump on bandwagons and, you know, follow trends. And so it's like a veneer, you know? We're doing this "hip-hop" thing. Certainly, there's commercialization, even in education. Oh, I've got this new curriculum, and it uses hip-hop. And so cautionary flags go up for me whenever somebody says that they use hip-hop, as, rather, rather than saying I'm, my work is informed by hip-hop. So, I worry that there are people who sort of dip in and dip out because it's trendy. And it's probably why I'm more likely to use the term youth culture because my understanding of culture as someone who studied anthropology is that it's always changing and evolving. So where it was ten years ago is not where it's going to be ten years later. And that's what I'm looking at. I'm looking at its evolution, its reinvention.
Kelly:	When I hear you talk about people using hip-hop as a veneer, it makes me think of work you have done around culturally relevant pedagogy where you critique individuals who enact it at a surface level. Do you kind of share the same concerns with

	hip-hop work that people may start to misunderstand the work because they have this freedom to kind of just flow in and out of hip-hop education at their leisure?
Dr. Ladson-Billings:	I mean, you know, one of the beauties of working in the academy is you get to study what you want to study. So I can't fault them for that. I'm someone who was, you know, sort of late to the party, and from that perspective, but I just want people to make a commitment, to study things deeply. You know, if it turns out that they develop another interest, that's fine, but I'm more concerned that people are doing very superficial things. And I would say the same thing around all of my culturally relevant pedagogy, you know, I don't recognize a lot of the stuff that people are doing under the rubric of culturally relevant pedagogy. I'm like, what? I didn't say anything like that. So, you know, you can't control it once you create something conceptual/theoretical and give it to the world what the world does with it. You know, I mean, we're having the same debate about critical race theory now, you know, [laugh], it, it is nothing like, yeah. Uh, the work that I spent over a year in the law library trying to understand.
Kelly:	How do we push back against that? When we go out into the world, how do we advocate for people who have an interest in hip-hop—which is like, that's dope, we want that, right?—but how do we encourage them to think deeper about hip-hop? What does that look like?
Dr. Ladson-Billings:	I think you have to trust young people. This is their movement. And we had to be willing to follow them in this movement. And I think almost any movement for liberation is going to have youth at its forefront. You know, we talk about Martin Luther King as if he were ancient. That brother is young. By the time he died, he was 39 when he went down there to Montgomery. I mean, so think about that youth have always been at the forefront of liberation, and I think we have to be willing to trust them.

While Dr. Ladson-Billings encourages educators to engage in hip-hop as a part of their lifelong learning as an educator, she cautions that the way we engage in this learning is important. When engaging with hip-hop, it is essential to recognize the origins and history of hip-hop and that hip-hop has five creative elements: MC, graffiti arts, b-boying/b-girling, DJ, and knowledge of self. This is particularly imperative when bringing hip-hop into educational spaces because hip-hop's element *knowledge of self* encourages participants of hip-hop culture to be aware and critical of who they are, be authentic to themselves and their identities, and be confident in themselves to make positive social-political change for their communities (Adjapong, 2017). If this understanding and cultivation of self are undertaken with critical care, then the potential for superficial implementations of hip-hop education are minimized significantly because one understands the sociopolitical importance of hip-hop to the communities that they are engaged with, as well as their role in the work. In transmitting this cautionary tale, Dr. Ladson-Billings believes there are ways to mitigate the potential of misappropriation in hip-hop education by interrogating hip-hop in relationship to education deeply and by trusting and allowing the youth to lead in educational spaces, which again requires the decentering of the educator/scholar.

Edmund: What is needed to move the field of hip-hop and education from mainly scholarship and theoretical applications to more practical applications?
In your thoughts might be necessary, to support white educators in particular, but all educators, right? Who may not have the skills? And I think it's probably similar to like the challenges that you've seen in relationship to culturally relevant pedagogy and how people make sense of your framework.

Dr. Ladson-Billings: You know, it may be indeed a, um, problem of canonization… when you begin to curate this stuff and, and make it more canonical, then the teachers have something that they can use. I just did a talk a couple of weeks ago for group of teachers in DC. And I talked to them about the fact that they're missing, mixing up the ingredients with the chef. I can only give them ingredients. Yeah. But if you don't know how to cook, you can really screw up stuff. Right? I gave them the example of my mother's mac and cheese. My mother made the absolute best mac and cheese in the entire extended family. And I don't care what the family gathering was. Someone would say, Jessie, are you going to bring the mac and cheese? Yeah, I got you. I have watched her. I have written it down. I have tried, I can't make the Mac and Cheese like her. I just can't. I, you know, but I've learned to make mac and cheese in my mother's deceased now, but I've learned to make mac and cheese that has the family saying, "Hey, you gonna make the mac and cheese?" It's different. But it's got the ingredients and I've often put my own spin on it. That's what has to happen in the classroom of a real teacher, but we don't have a lot of chefs. We got some cooks, we got some short-order cooks, but we don't have people who creatively say, you know what, I'm missing this ingredient, but I'm going to swap this out and put this in here. Oh, I got this group of folks in here. I gotta switch up this. Those people are not there in number. Yeah. We just got people who think they can just read the cookbook and produce it. And, and, and you can't.

A key experience in evolving from a "short order cook" to a "chef" is the ability to try innovative things, but today's educational climate does not always allow this freedom for educators. The passage of No Child Left Behind, and subsequent accountability measures like Race to the Top and the Every Child Succeeds Act, have led to an increase in high-stakes standardized testing (Au, 2016; Ravitch, 2016). Failure to show improved test scores meant that the federal government could strip schools of federal funding and initiate school takeovers (Au, 2016). These high-stakes consequences have pressured teachers into adopting pedagogy and curriculum that aims to increase student test scores, which often means relinquishing control of the curriculum and adopting pedagogical techniques that seek to deposit knowledge into students so they can regurgitate the content on the next test. For example, Au (2007) found that high-stakes standardized testing narrowed the curriculum students received to focus on tested content, and teachers increased the use of teacher-centered pedagogy. However, teachers have felt tension with the pressure to conform to standardized testing, and many desire to embody the level of innovation Dr. Ladson-Billings describes. However, Shelton & Brooks (2018) found that standardized testing hampered teachers' desire to be innovative, and time constraints allowed little time for teachers to delve into topics their students were interested in. Further hampering teacher desires to be innovative, Santoro (2018) found that teachers regularly found their desires to be creative and to inspire students did not align with the standardized testing expectations they were expected to adhere to. The current educational climate around standardized testing does not allow for the time and freedom necessary for teachers to hone in on the art of teaching truly; instead, the current climate encourages the production of "short-order cooks" that regurgitate curricular and pedagogical toolkits.

Dr. Ladson-Billings: I also think we have to give [teachers] the opportunity to grow. I mean, this is one of these professions where we think people (I'll push this, this chef metaphor a little bit) you're coming out of culinary school. You, you are not the chef. You're going to be five years down the road. You know, some stuff, but you're going to learn some stuff about the way real kitchens operate and restaurants operate and what's considered a signature dish at this place. And you know, certain things you don't mess with…

so a part of it is how do we, how do we help teachers grow into this role as teachers? And another thing I've been talking about is the degree to which, I feel in some professions you can have, you have to have zero tolerance for so-called bad apples. I always give people the example, if I go to the airport and the gate agent says, well, you know, we have a few bad apples in our cockpits these days. Oh, I'm going home. I'm not getting on that plane. There is a zero tolerance for bad actors, bad apples as pilots—it's life and death. Yeah. I feel it should be that same way about police officers. You know, the way that we shrug our shoulders and say, well, there's always a few bad. No, if you get, if the society has given you the right to carry a weapon and you have life and death at your hip, or you can't be a bad actor. Yeah, yeah. Not at all, do something else. I have the audacity to believe the same thing about teaching. Yeah. That we can't, you, you actually have life and death too. It's over a longer span. But you have it at your fingertips. So no, *we can't. Our kids can't survive bad teachers.*

Edmund: I agree. This has been an amazing conversation. OG, if you can radically dream about the future of hip-hop and education, what would you envision?

Dr. Ladson-Billings: Well, I think I would envision a kind of merging between young people's out-of-school time and in-school time. You know, I've been saying to people in this pandemic moment that we have to stop talking about after school, there is no after school. I like what we're doing at the Sacramento area youth speaks, we decided we're pushing into schools. We're not waiting for school to be over. We're coming to school. We are coming into English classes. We are working directly with kids. So many of the things that we think that we can do after school, to me, the future is that we push into schools that we begin to work side by side, with educators, with quote certified educators, and that we create a much more organic experience for kids. Not necessarily a formal one, but one in which we get to touch each and every kid in a variety of settings. I just think we have to sort of saturate the educational experience for young people....I'm excited because I think our young people can lead us in this way...and if we would just, you know, not be so afraid to let go, to let our young people show us what it is that they are bringing to the table and lead us. Yeah, we'll be just fine.

Throughout this chapter, we highlighted the importance of educators decentering themselves with the goal of gaining a deeper understanding of their students, school community, and hip-hop culture. Dr. Ladson-Billings highlights that there are necessary shifts that we must consider in regard to teacher induction. Teachers are often expected to be experts once they enter their classrooms once graduating from teacher preparation programs, but new teachers are in dire need of support in acclimating to schools and overall school communities. In addition to teachers receiving professional development in regard to their content area, novice and veteran teachers should be trained to understand the complexities, challenges and successes of the surrounding community. This training can happen in partnership with local community members but requires educators to recognize the community cultural wealth (Yosso, 2005) that has always existed with local school communities. Further, it requires communities to be compensated for their support of local schools as this can demonstrate the value that local communities have in relation to educational institutions. This brings us to consider, Dr. Ladson-Billings' radical dream for the future of hip-hop and education, which includes a vision for an increase of community and school partnerships with the goal of merging youths out of school lives and experiences with educational programming. Historically, traditional teaching strategies and school curricula have been anchored in western views and Eurocentric frameworks that position whiteness as the center of legitimate knowledge, and as a result, other knowledge as peripheral and insignificant (Baker, 2012; Lynch, 2018). Schools across the country do not reflect the needs of culturally diverse groups in regard to curricula, pedagogy, and school design. By providing opportunities for community members to collaborate with traditionally certified educators on programming, school culture, and climate, we are creating the context for students out of school lives to merge with their educational pursuits.

To learn more about Dr. Gloria Ladson-Billings's research and scholarship, check out the following:

- Ladson-Billings, G. (2021). Culturally relevant pedagogy: Asking a different question. Teachers College Press.
- Ladson-Billings, G. (2017). The (r)evolution will not be standardized: Teacher education, hip-hop pedagogy, and culturally relevant pedagogy 2.0. *Culturally sustaining pedagogies: Teaching and learning for justice in a changing world*, 141–156.
- Ladson-Billings, G. (2018). From big homie the OG, to GLB: Hip-Hop and the reinvention of a pedagogue. In # *HipHopEd: The compilation on hip-hop education* (pp. 21–26). Brill.

References

Au, W. (2016). Meritocracy 2.0: High-stakes, standardized testing as a racial project of neoliberal multiculturalism. *Educational Policy, 30*(1), 39–62.

Au, W. (2007). High-stakes testing and curricular control: A qualitative metasynthesis. *Educational Researcher, 36*(5), 258–267. https://www.jstor.org/stable/30137912

Baker, M. (2012). Modernity/coloniality and eurocentric education: Towards a post-occidental self-understanding of the present. *Policy Futures in Education, 10*(1), 4–22.

Greene, M. (2007). Imagination and becoming (Bronx charter school of the arts). Retrieved June 4, 2009.

Lynch, M. E. (2018). The hidden nature of whiteness in education: Creating active allies in White teachers. *Journal of Educational Supervision, 1*(1). https://doi.org/10.31045/jes.1.1.2.

Ravitch, D. (2016). *The death and life of the American school system: How testing and choice are undermining education.* Basic Books.

Santoro, D. A. (2018). *Demoralized: Why teachers leave the profession they love and how they can stay.* Harvard Education Press.

Shelton, S. A., & Brooks, T. (2019). "We Need to Get These Scores Up": A narrative examination of the challenges of teaching literature in the age of standardized testing. *Journal of Language and Literacy Education, 15*(2), 1–17.

· 2 ·

INTENTIONAL CENTERING OF HIP-HOP WITHIN AND BEYOND EDUCATIONAL SPACES: KEEPING IT REAL WITH P. THANDI HICKS HARPER

Dr. P. Thandi Hicks Harper is the founder and president of Youth Popular Culture Institute, a non-profit organization that utilizes hip-hop culture to foster positive public health within historically marginalized communities. Dr. Hicks Harper's work focuses on public health systems and youth development as she designed a research-based curriculum, Hip-Hop 2 Prevent Substance Abuse and HIV, that is implemented in schools and communities across the nation.

Edmund: When you engage in research and community work, what groups do you primarily focus on and with/for?

Dr. Hicks Harper: I primarily work for myself in the best interests of children, families, and communities, particularly those Black and Brown young people who are marginalized. I engage a lot with the federal government in the areas of health education and the areas of prevention, specifically substance use prevention. I have engaged with scholars all over the country, working to figure out how to engage young people so that they are intrinsically motivated to choose healthy lifestyles. I work with local governments and state governments as a part of the hip-hop to prevent curriculum that I developed along with others. I'm engaged with folks in the Northeast Delta of Louisiana, Houston, Seattle, Baltimore, North

Edmund: Carolina, and Houston. There are various organizations that I engage with regarding health and youth development.

Edmund: I think what's unique about you and your position from the other folks we interviewed for this book is that you are based within the community, and I love how you are based within the community and are working with large and also influential, and impactful community organizations. We want to highlight the importance of hip-hop work in community spaces as well, and we want folks to understand that hip-hop education doesn't only exist in academic spaces. So, tell us what brought you to like, thinking about conceptualizing and leveraging hip-hop in community-based work as it relates to education, and what motivates you to continue in this work?

Dr. Hicks Harper: I've always been radical in my thinking. In the 1970s and 1980s, I was teaching elementary school, and I wanted to bring hip-hop into the classroom, particularly, because I had this radical dream that hip-hop could work in the classroom because it was working with the development of my son, who was trying to be a rapper. So, he was looking at sources, looking at the dictionary, getting excited about words trying to write rhymes, even if the use of words didn't always make sense—it rhymed. Even though I had admittedly kind of had disdain for hip-hop as an educator, as a revolutionary person, and as someone who recognizes the value of things that I might not understand, I said I needed to tune into hip-hop. I needed to understand what was going on. My experience with my son is what propelled me to try to use hip-hop in my classroom.

As an educator, I always thought there needed to be a revolution in education. Young people do not always focus on their experience with education, they're often trying to get a good grade, and learning is more than just getting a grade. How do we get students engaged in the content, and what are the ideas that we trying to communicate to them? So that's what got me going in terms of, let me take a look at it and let me see how, how it can work. And that meant me moving away from the traditional methods.

Dr. Hicks Harper explains that she began exploring the use of hip-hop within educational spaces during the 1970s and 1980s because her son introduced her to the art form. Dr. Hicks Harper recognized that her son was engaged in hip-hop because it led him to pick up a dictionary and look up sources that supported him in writing his hip-hop rhymes. Although admittedly, Dr. Hicks Harper had a disdain toward hip-hop originally, as an educator, she couldn't deny its possible benefit within educational spaces, which encouraged her to incorporate hip-hop in her elementary school classroom. During her time as an elementary educator in the 70s and 80s, Dr. Hicks Harper recognized that students were not being engaged in school by the use of traditional teaching methods, which led her to explore the use of hip-hop in educational spaces. It's important to recognize that educators and community members have and continue to utilize hip-hop without having a platform or possibly an interest in sharing their methods and approaches with the larger community, as academics would. Educators and community members who utilize hip-hop in their respective spaces also deserve their flowers for exploring the utilization of youth culture within educational spaces. Here, Dr. Hicks Harper recognizes hip-hop as a tool to support engagement, but later in her career explores the use of hip-hop to support the development of youth.

> **Dr. Hicks Harper:** My research centered around hip-hop and education goes way back to a DMX concert. I will never forget that I went to a DMX concert and then had cassette recorders to record the show and responses from young people. So, with my cassette recorder, I'll sit with some young people next to me to ask and understand why they like DMX, whether DMX has any messages they like, and so forth. Researching has always been a part of what I, love to do, especially when it comes from the mouths and perspectives of young people. It's just what I do. Then I decided that I would go to college, continue my education because I had a Bachelor's degree, and get my Master's from Howard university, then my Ph.D. from The University of Maryland College Park, because I wanted a seat at the table. I wanted to be at the table so that folks would listen to me. A Ph.D. was a prerequisite of it. You had to have some credentials behind your name for folks who really listen to you. And so that's what I did. I went back to school, and then they said I had to reference everybody—like Maslow, Vygotsky, Piaget, Eric Ericson, and all those guys because I was talking about hip-hop culture, and nothing was out there at the time, so I had to use theories of anthropology. So, I had to reference, like, you know, Margaret Mead and Kottak and some of those other ones. This is why hip-hop development, the theoretical framework, came about, because I'm like, I don't want to keep referencing these people.

Dr. Hicks Harper explains the necessity of gaining credentials in research and education (doctorate) to "have a seat at the table" to share her research and youth perspectives on the power and benefit of hip-hop in educational spaces. This a tension that many scholars, classroom teachers, and community educators possess a deeply personal, social, and cultural connection to the hip-hop experience because they want to seek higher education as a way to uplift youth and their community. This is seen in how Dr. Hicks Harper leveraged her research knowledge to capture youth perspectives about hip-hop, specifically DMX's music. Further, those who embark on academic journeys with the intention of uplifting youth and community voices are encouraged and often forced to cite social-cultural theorists whose work doesn't include or directly speak to historically marginalized groups that hip-hop culture gives voice. Dr. Hicks Harper's experience with being directed to cite predominantly white scholars whose work vaguely speaks to her research is echoed by many Black women academics. Black women academics have always occupied a unique place within academia where they are expected to conform to white frameworks and understandings in academic spaces even if those frameworks and perspectives do not speak to their experiences (hooks, 2015; Lorde, 2009). The pull Dr. Hicks Harper felt to create her own framework that reflected not only her perspective but the perspectives of the hip-hop populations she was engaged with. While this tension is often discussed by Black women academics through a Black feminist lens, it is found in broader discussions of Black education as well. Tillman (2002) articulates this tension in regard to Black education, noting that "there is a need to consider research frameworks that can help researchers to more fully capture the experiences of African Americans, their struggles as well as their successes" (p. 3). Existing frameworks that traditionally derive meaning from white individuals' perspectives and experiences simply do not, and cannot, capture the nuances of the Black experience, leaving a void in what the field of education understands about the Black experience in education (Dillard, 2000; Boykin, 1994; Tillman, 2002). Further, Marc Lamont Hill and Emery Petchauer (2013) express the need for scholars engaged in hip-hop and education research to develop new methodological approaches, locate new units of analysis, address broader policy concerns, and explore gaps in hip-hop education literature to fully realize the potential of hip-hop education.

> **Dr. Hicks Harper:** That's where hip-hop development came about. I began to really put some things down, my thoughts and everything and put things down and then go back to Africa, look at the nine dimensions of the African worldview to look at those dimensions and juxtapose them to hip-hop culture. I saw similarities. I'm like, whoa, this needs to be the foundation of the hip-hop development theory because I'm a strong believer that hip-hop development is human

> development. When you relate it to young people, hip-hop development is youth development. I mean, that's how you successfully engage young people, and I am really excited that with the paper reality pedagogy and hip-hop spoke word therapy those interventions, we were able to use hip-hop development as a framework for discussing how successful they have been in classrooms and in counseling sessions.

Dr. Hicks Harper's conceptualization of Hip-Hop Development "speaks to hip-hop's ability to provide the context, core components, and practical applications necessary for positive youth development, information-processing, and successful social and emotional learning" (Hicks Harper & Emdin, 2022, p. 103). Hip-Hop Development outlines nine root elements that represent African belief and value systems, as articulated by Boykin (1983), and applies them to hip-hop's role in education. Hicks Harper and Emdin (2022) describe these nine root elements:

1. Spirituality—Value for the not always observable. Respecting the significance of soul, faith, hope, light, ancestry, authenticity, spiritual intelligence, and possibilities.
2. Harmony—Value is placed on the positive psycho-sociocultural connectedness among natal and extended family members/crews as they exist in mutual or distant environments.
3. Movement—Value is placed on rhythm, as it exists in life—physically, mentally, and spiritually.
4. Verve—Value is placed on vigor, energy, and enthusiasm.
5. Affect—Value is placed on the relevance of emotion and passion.
6. Communalism—Value is placed on the "we" more than the "I."
7. Expressive Individualism—Value is placed on individual styles of expression and their meanings. Individualism is valued for its support of the collective.
8. Orality—Value is placed on holding the oral tradition in high esteem.
9. Social Time Perspective—Value is placed on open-ended engagement, regardless of time.

Hicks Harper (2007) contends that Hip-Hop Development is an effective framework for individuals who are interested in incorporating hip-hop culture into youth involvement, leadership, and cognitive development and processing. The framework for Hip-Hop Development has been utilized in education and community health prevention programming as it allows youth to bring their realities, ideas, choices, and communication styles to the forefront for positive change.

Kelly: Earlier, you said when you go to these conferences, it's your goal to make sure that hip-hop is on the agenda—wherever you are. Even if you can't be in that space, why is it essential for hip-hop to be discussed?

Dr. Hicks Harper: Well, it's important that hip-hop education and health are on the agendas because not enough folks are talking about it. We are beginning to talk about it, but folks are still not sure. They're not sure how to approach it. They're not sure what hip-hop is. Some of the conferences that I go to, some people, very surprisingly, still think hip-hop is for Blacks only, or it's, it's just gangster, or it is just full of profanity and, and, you know, misogynistic. They don't see what I call formal features of hip-hop culture. This is important to me because a lot of folks still don't get it, but they want to act as if they get it. They just think of music. So, you know, it's, it's up to us as hip-hop scholars, as hip-hop activists, as hip-hop laypersons, as young people engaged in hip-hop—it's up to us—to make sure that people really understand what hip-hop education is.

But if I can get back to Hip-Hop Development theoretical framework for a second, there are some, there are these nine roots, right? These nine roots, which are the core components that must be valued and acknowledged, must be AKUVA. That means *acknowledged, known, understood, valued, and applied*, right? They have to be AKUVA in order for successful youth engagement to take place. So now we're focusing on hip-hop and our culture. And as I mentioned before, these come from these nine dimensions that represent the African worldview. So, we're radically dreaming about the future of hip-hop and education, right? So, I see these nine roots being AKUVA and classrooms all over the world. If these nine roots are being AKUVA, and I argue at least seven of them, we're talking about spirituality, communalism, harmony, social time perspective, morality, verve, and movement effect. If these can be valued in places where we engage young people, where we value that spirit, we value what they bring in there. Some things must be processed mentally, right? That we value and use these things in creative ways. Like I know the work and whether it's mix tape creation or lyrical writing, or however creatively we want to do it right. That I almost would put my life on it, that there's going to be some more success when it comes to youth academic achievement.

Dr. Hicks Harper acknowledges that when engaging with the public and sharing her work around hip-hop development and hip-hop education folks truly do not understand hip-hop culture, although they have the perception that they do. Everyone who engages in hip-hop culture has some type of relationship with hip-hop, as even those who engage in hip-hop passively have a subjective view of the culture that is influenced by their personal feelings and opinions. While subjective views and understandings of hip-hop culture are necessary and demonstrate a relationship with hip-hop culture, in order to effectively utilize hip-hop within educational spaces, educators must also have an objective view of hip-hop culture that is influenced by facts and literal understandings of the culture. Having an objective view of hip-hop culture allows educators to be able to critique, challenge, and identify the nuance and practicality of hip-hop culture within educational spaces. For example, educators should have an understanding of the history of hip-hop and the context in which the culture was birthed so they can understand that hip-hop is radical and is anchored in social justice, innovation, and resiliency at its core and this must be exemplified in their practice. Further, Dr. Hicks Harper explains that educators and practitioners must AKUVA (*acknowledge, know, understand, value, and apply*) hip-hop to succeed in its use for youth development. Applying AKUVA requires an acknowledgment of the effectiveness of hip-hop within educational spaces, knowledge of the origins and history of hip-hop, an understanding of the nuances and complexities of hip-hop, demonstrating the value of hip-hop within educational spaces, and effectively applying hip-hop within educational spaces are all necessary for utilizing hip-hop in youth development in schools and community spaces. This is a concept Dr. Hicks Harper has been grappling with since she began considering the potential of hip-hop in education.

Dr. Hicks Harper: You know, and it was a dream. I was I felt like I was on the telephone with you guys or something, but it was a dream. I journal all the time, and I've been journaling for years. And I looked at my journal maybe about three weeks ago, my journal from 2019 or 2018. And it said, it said, I hope that hip-hop development will be recognized in by folks doing hip-hop work, hip-hop education work to the point where folks will realize how great it is, not how great I am, but how great the theory of change is and begin to use it in their writing and referencing it so that other people use it. Yeah. Now, that was 2018. Right? And today, this was a radical dream. I was like, I don't know how the heck this going to happen, but today that's really happening. It's beginning to take off, you know, it's like you can't miss when you dream. Cause your dream is a reflection of, your thoughts. What, when you're thinking, whatever you think about on a consistent basis is going to come back around. And I believe positively if it's positive, but you know, positive thoughts reflect positive thoughts that it's going to happen. The universe is going to make it happen. There's no question about it. I am not only doing you believe it, but I've also seen it just happen, right? Like we can't be, we got to be non-negotiable in this work. Regardless of what anybody says, we have got to stay true to the dream until it germinates; that means being consistent in our efforts, being consistent in publishing, if it's self-published on Instagram or Twitter, wherever it is, right? We got to publish even that, which we think might be least important, but relates to hip-hop and education. Somebody will take that thought, call you and say, let's publish something about it, or say, you know, you are right on it. And, and it becomes, it becomes a manifested, one's dream reality.

Dr. Hicks Harper's dream is for individuals to recognize the importance of the hip-hop development framework, a framework that encourages individuals engaged with youth to consider how hip-hop can support youth development. To really understand the significance of Dr. Hicks Harper's dream, it is imperative to recognize when she started this work and how long she has been committed to utilizing hip-hop across educational spaces. Dr. Hicks Harper published her first hip-hop education paper, "Rap music + education: The missing connection in the urban school system," in 1989. Dr. Hicks Harper (1989) argued that educators must seriously consider the potential of hip-hop to engage urban students—in the paper, which is often regarded as the first time hip-hop was acknowledged in educational spaces. Beyond being noted as one of the first in education to begin advocating for the use of hip-hop, Dr. Hicks Harper entered into the field during a time when conversations around hip-hop culture rarely acknowledged the potential of hip-hop; rather, academic institutions in the 1980s–1990s refused to see hip-hop as anything more than a rebellious and controversial fad that, wasn't deserving of serious examination (Dyson, 2004). The negative and dismissive attitudes around hip-hop during this time make Dr. Hicks Harper's (1989) centering of hip-hop in education all the more powerful. Further, the fact that Dr. Hicks Harper continues to say this same message today stands as a call to action for anyone curious about the potential of hip-hop in education. Dr. Hicks Harper shares her radical dream, which she released into the world many years ago, which is finally beginning to manifest now. Dr. Hicks Harper's journey is a demonstration of why it's important for hip-hop scholars and educators to employ a radical imagination as it relates to hip-hop and education work and then work towards manifesting that radical dream. Many hip-hop educators and scholars, even today, struggle with convincing people to find value in their work and finding appropriate outlets and funding for their work. In spite of these challenges, we must persist in identifying new visions for what we want hip-hop and education to embody even if they do not currently exist. This is a key component of freedom dreaming, in which Kelley posits that "without new visions, we don't know what to build, only what to knock down. We not only end up confused, rudderless, and cynical, but we forget that making a revolution is not a series of clever maneuvers and tactics but a process that can and must transform us" (2022, p. xii). If we are collectively radically imagining and working towards creating new visions of spaces that uplift and privilege hip-hop and education work, we are moving towards the goal of creating increased opportunities for hip-hop to be utilized across educational spaces.

To learn more about Dr. Thandi Hicks Harper's research and scholarship, check out the following:

- Hicks Harper, P. T., & Emdin, C. (2022). Cultivating science genius through hip-hop development and reality pedagogy. *Diversity in Higher Education, 25,* 99–113. https://doi.org/10.1108/S1479-36442022000 0025008.
- Hicks Harper, P. T. (2020). Hip-Hop development: The roots of positive youth development and engagement in education and health prevention. In E. Adjapong & I. Levy (Eds.), *#HipHopEd: The compilation on hip-hop education* (Vol. 2). Peter Lang Publishing.
- Hicks Harper, P. T., Rhodes, W. A., Tomas, D. E., Leary, G., & Quinton, S. L. (2007). Hip-Hop development bridging the generational divide for youth development. *Journal of Youth Development, 2*(2), 1–14. https://doi.org/10.5195/jyd.2007.345.

References

Boykin, A. W. (1983). The academic performance of Afro-American children. In J. Spence (Ed.), *Achievement and achievement motives* (pp. 324–371). W. H. Freeman.

Dillard, C. (2000). The substance of things hoped for, the evidence of things not seen: Examining an endarkened feminist epistemology in educational research and leadership. *International Journal of Qualitative Studies in Education, 13*(6), 661–681.

Dyson, M. E. (2004). *The Michael Eric Dyson Reader*. Civitas Books.

Hicks Harper, P. T. (1989). Rap music + education: The missing connection in the urban school system in LD productions, *Rap Attack '89: Rapping for a Cause Rap Conference Journal*. Trump Regency, Atlantic City, NJ. Available from the Youth Popular Culture Institute: MD.

Hicks Harper, P. T., & Emdin, C. (2022). Cultivating science genius through hip-hop development and reality pedagogy. *Diversity in Higher Education, 25*, 99–113. https://doi.org/10.1108/S1479-364420220000025008.

Hicks Harper, P. T., Rhodes, W. A., Thomas, D. E., Leary, G., & Quinton, E. S. (2007). Hip-Hop development: Bridging the generational divide for youth development. *Journal of Youth Development—Bridging Research and Practice, 2*(2), 43–55.

Hill, M. L., & Petchauer, E. (2013). *Schooling hip-hop: Expanding hip-hop based education across the curriculum*. Teachers College Press.

hooks, b. (2015). *Feminist theory: From margin to center*. Routledge.

Kelley, R. D. (2022). *Freedom dreams: The black radical imagination*. Beacon Press.

Lorde, A. (2009). Poet as teacher—Human as poet—Teacher as human. In R. P. Byrd, J. B. Cole & B. Guy-Sheftall (Eds.), *I am your sister: Collected and unpublished writings of Audre Lorde* (pp. 182–183). New York, NY: Oxford University Press.

Tillman, L. C. (2002). Culturally sensitive research approaches: An African-American perspective. *Educational Researcher, 31*(9), 3–12. https://www.jstor.org/stable/3594490

· 3 ·

INTERROGATING ANTI-BLACKNESS IN RELATIONSHIP TO HIP-HOP: KEEPING IT REAL WITH IAN LEVY

Dr. Ian Levy is an assistant professor and program director of school counseling at Manhattan College. His research examines hip-hop informed practices in schools as a culturally responsive approach to counseling wherein students process difficult thoughts and feelings through the writing, recording, and performing emotionally themed music. Levy formally served as a high school counselor, where he started exploring the use of hip-hop in school counseling settings and developed a framework for Hip-Hop and Spoken Work Therapy.

Edmund: What is your personal experience with hip-hop culture, and how has the culture impacted you?

Dr. Ian Levy: I always liked hip-hop, but I grew up in a family where hip-hop was not viewed as real music, and so hip-hop was always like this taboo thing. It was like, oh, it's not real music. I remember the first time I heard Lil Wayne's The Carter 3. And I was like, you know, nearing the end of high school, like something like that, I think. And I was just like, it was amazing. I had a roommate who was like this dope freestyler, and every morning I'd wake up, and he'd be playing like tribe beats and like day loss, soul instrumentals, and just like rhyming in the living room of our apartment in Queens. And I used to just join him for fun. And then because he would then have friends over who would start rhyming with him, you know, in our apartment when I'd get home from class or whatever, I would start writing rhymes regularly. I just kind of fell into writing and rhyming with roommates in this apartment in Queens and listening to hip-hop and talking about hip-hop in this space. And that, that was for me where I really started to, like, I guess, understand how to create lyrics. I was writing without thinking about a lot of things that I had not talked about. I had a learning disability growing up in high school, and as I wrote, I was writing rhymes about that. Right. I was writing rhymes about, like, you know, just, I had some medical challenges growing up too. And so, I just was writing about a lot of that in my rhymes and like sharing that in this dorm room or in this apartment rather. And like the roommates were just loving up on me. And that, for me, was really transformative because it made me wanna write more. It made me want to explore myself more. It made me want to keep coming back and sharing more, you know?

Edmund: Yeah. What I hear from you is that hip-hop, like, your early experience or your introduction to hip-hop, should I say like, was it like it created an affirming space for you and like, and your identities and how you existed in the world. So, talk about that experience.

Dr. Ian Levy: So that's the piece, right? So, like, I felt like I was able to express all of who I was through lyric writing in these spaces and my peers were as well, and I was able to learn about them. It just felt like a natural fit. When you think about counseling work in schools, the most general approaches to counseling were built for and by White folks. They were not built to engage Black and Brown youth. And so hip-hop just seemed like, naturally, counseling. It seemed like, authentically, this thing. So, the first thought for me was like, I just want to bring a little microphone into my office, put it up in the corner, and just like talk about songs that youth like, write some rhymes with them, learn more about who they are.

Like many scholars and practitioners who engage in hip-hop education research and praxis, Dr. Levy research in school counseling is informed by his personal experiences with hip-hop (Hill, 2013). Dr. Levy's introduction to writing lyrics with his college roommates contributed to his positive experience with hip-hop, which allowed him to connect with a positive cognitive and emotive process and facilitated his passion for school counseling. In his research, Levy demonstrates that lyric writing historically has been a tool for cognitive and emotive journaling, found effective in group and individual counseling as a medium to foster self-awareness, emotional reflection, the restructuring of thoughts, and as a stress-coping tactic (Levy, 2019). Through Dr. Levy's positive experiences with hip-hop, he empowered to create opportunities for adolescents to have similar opportunities to engage in emotional reflection through lyric writing.

Dr. Ian Levy: There are community-defined practices that are, that are in hip-hop that already function in some capacity as a form of counseling or at least catharsis for folks. And so, it's the job of school counselors to learn about what those are and then use those in their work to elevate the theories that they've been given.

Well, lyric writing, for example, is one of the tenants of my hip-hop and school counseling model. Lyric writing capitalizes on the fact that like folks who engage with hip-hop have always used journals or the notepad on a phone or something like that. So there's like the references to the, to the documenting life experiences through lyrics. So, one of the tenants then is the use of lyric writing is what, what I've called emotive and cognitive journaling. And that's pulling from like some cognitive behavioral approaches and counseling and some person-centered or humanistic approaches to counseling and basically asks students to reflect between counseling sessions on a given emotional experience or behavior. So, if they're like, you know, they got tension at home with a parent, and they always get in arguments with their parents. And it always results in them running out of the house or cursing them out, or something happens every time they're home. And they get frustrated with their parent. I want them to go into their room and throw on their headphones. I've emailed them a beat that is thematically aligned with anger or frustration or sadness, or whatever emotion we've identified. And then, they can flush out rhymes at that moment using that mechanism that they already use of documenting lived experience through rhyme. Like do that, and then bring that rhyme back to the next session. Right. So lyric writing is an ongoing way of tracking specific behaviors or feelings that we have identified in our sessions as necessary.

Collaboration is another element, which is just simply pulling on the fact that people collaborate. When you collaborate with somebody, you got to learn all about who they are. So, you can make a like fire track together. And that's what happens in studios, right? Like you go to the studios, and you learn a million things about a person that you might not have known when you're making a track. And so, because we know that we can strategically pair youth together who we know are in dealing with similar concerns and say, "Hey, I want you to write a track about, you know, grief together. So come through, I got a fire a beat, and I want you to work together. And by doing that, I'm trusting that they're going to know how to ask each other questions about their content. They're going to know how to push each other, to share with each other about what it is that they've experienced because the goal is creating a cohesive song. So again, it's like, it's just trusting in the collaboration, but like focusing it on this idea of role-playing and like being able to talk through your situation with another person, learn from other people, prepare for future situations, all that stuff. But like through roleplay.

Mixtape making, there's a couple more mixtape making is broader than all of this, right? So, like, while these are individual lyric writing sort of activities like collaboration, emotive journaling or mixtape making are a group process. And so, when I'm working within a small, in small group counseling settings, or even potentially in classroom settings, I can engage a large group of folks in the co-construction of a mixtape, a collection of songs around a shared theme. So, like if, if youth have decided and youth can decide, they always decide what that theme is. So, I've had youth construct mixtapes of, like, about policing. We did a mixtape last year around the, or two years ago, rather around the insurrection in the capital. And then more largely like, just like the state of America politically. So, what that does is it allows groups of youth to all write songs about their own experiences relevant to that theme. So, it creates sort of a shared process where we're all working as a group towards creating a theme. It's aligned with youth participatory action research. So, youth are doing research, they're reading articles, but they're learning about this issue comprehensively, reflecting on who they are and how they feel about the issue. And then constructing songs through creating a project and then disseminating that through like listening parties and, you know, or putting songs up on SoundCloud or music videos or whatever the group decides. But it's this group counseling process that is aligned inherently with mixtape making, which guesses what does all of those things anyway if you're going to link with a bunch of people and, and create a mixtape, you have to go through a lot of those processes.

Lastly, creating school studios with youth as places for healing because there's something about that studio. When you walk in, the dim lighting and the vibe in the space encourage you to want to express yourself. Talk about studios as these transformative spaces where they can really go through sort of the emotional labor required to create something really powerful that resonates with an audience. So, if we're doing emotional work and we're trying to create things that resonate with us and people that hear it and to transform ourselves, then why not engage youth in the co-creation of studios because youth know what makes them feel comfortable? So, trusting youth to design their own spaes, to engage in all of the hip-hop work.

And so that's the framework, but it's deeply connected to things that I would argue and how argued already happen in hip-hop. So it's not, I don't even feel like it's like this ingenious thing that I did, or it's just like this is happening in hip-hop. Yeah. Like, let's just do this work in schools and be thoughtful about it and trust that youth are going to like take it to where it needs to go.

Dr. Ian Levy's research focuses on designing and implementing youth center counseling practices that are anchored in hip-hop practices. As he describes above, his work aligns hip-hop cultural practices with counseling strategies to support youth in having culturally responsive experiences while engaging in counseling interventions. Dr. Levy designed and researched his framework for Hip-Hop and Spoken Work Therapy (HHSWT), which is a counseling model whereby youth engage in previously validated counseling interventions through the process of writing, recording, and performing hip-hop music (Levy, 2012). Dr. Levy argues that HHPWT invites school counselors to identify hip-hop cultural practices that their students might experience or engage in within their communities to use for catharsis during counseling sessions. Specifically, HHSWT offers school counselors a set of hip-hop-centered activities and/or tools that they can use in the counseling process to support youth in exploring difficult thoughts and feelings. HHSWT acknowledges that most therapy and counseling frameworks were designed without consideration of the cultural diversity of potential clients and leverages hip-hop practices to support youth and communities who regularly engage in hip-hop culture. Further, HHSWT supports the need for culturally responsive approaches to counseling by centering hip-hop, a Black culture and art form, as Black Americans in the United States are noted to use mental health services less than other racial/ethnic groups and are typically underrepresented in voluntary mental health care (Cummings & Druss, 2011).

Kelly: How do you envision Hip-Hop and Spoken Work Therapy as being something that mental health professionals can implement? Because the reality is a lot of counselors may not be as comfortable as you are sitting with students and spitting rhymes, right? So how do you support them?

Dr. Ian Levy: How do we do it? Yeah. So, great question. One that I'm admittedly working through, right? I'll give you my thoughts on it, but like I have certainly not figured this thing out yet by any stretch. But I think people that don't understand hip-hop or that are, like, think that they can't do hip-hop because they don't know how to rhyme or something like that. Like how do we respond to those folks?

So, I don't believe that you have to practice an element to do this work. I just want to put that out there. And I know that that's, like, some people might believe that that's necessary. I don't. And the reason I don't is because if we really want to implement this, about 80% of school counselors are White women. So, if we know that most of the people that are engaged in this work don't understand what hip-hop is and we want to implement it largely, then we can't put exclusionary criteria. Like you have to be able to rhyme, or you have to be able to do this, to engage everybody.

What you do have to be able to do is understand and appreciate what hip-hop is. It's this deep appreciation. How do you cultivate a deep appreciation for hip-hop? Well, if we know that young people are already writing rhymes on their phones, can I listen to the rhyme? Can I say, "Hey, share that with me," and listen to it? A big part of how that begins for me is like really working on listening to hip-hop on your own, getting your own playlists of like top hip-hop songs, and engaging in your own listening. But then I look at student lyrics, highlight lyrics, have a conversation about what we think the student meant by this lyric, learn to dissect lyrics, understand the underlying emotional content, the underlying cognitive content and get so comfortable in it. How do you engage in this really deeply, like listening and conversing around the content? I think that that needs to be the focus of the preparation. I don't need to teach somebody how to rhyme. I don't need to teach somebody how to use a recording software to do this work.

I also think it's a fair ask to have folks go to hip-hop spaces in their community that is open, right? Like, don't be creepy and show up to things that aren't open, but like go find open mic nights, find some concerts, like go listen and go observe, and then reflect for yourself and reflect yourself: what do I like about the space? What are some of the things that are rubbing me the wrong way that maybe are preventing me from appreciating this space? So it's like deep self-work around it, and I think cultivating a deep appreciation for hip-hop culture is what is required to be successful in this work.

For Dr. Levy, an understanding of the historical underpinnings of hip-hop is essential in implementing hip-hop education. Hip-Hop is a culture that was created organically by Black, Latinx, and immigrant communities in the Bronx during a socio-economic crisis during the 1970s (Chang, 2007; Rose, 1994). Further, hip-hop continues to be innovated by Black and brown youth, particularly within urban centers and has also proven to have effective applications within educational spaces. Because hip-hop is a culture that was created by marginalized communities, it is important that educators center and respect this reality when engaging hip-hop in their practice (Adjapong & Allen, 2023). The understanding of this history is imperative because it is this understanding and subsequent critique and reflection of practice that will ensure that we are not replicating similar systems and structures that hip-hop was created to counter. This task is potentially magnified for white educators.

Kelly: What does that look like then to get particularly White educators engaged in this work with integrity and urgency? Because when I hear you talk about encouraging them to get into hip-hop spaces, it's like, "Yeah! You need to be familiar with the culture and things like that." But how do we do that in a way that doesn't make it seem like this is like a zoo safari, and we're going to examine this exotic culture, you know what I mean? So, what does that look like for you, because it's a fine line…

Dr. Ian Levy: 100%. It's a fine line between and appropriation.

Kelly: Yeah! Talk about that a little bit.

Dr. Ian Levy: Yeah, yeah, yeah. It's such a fine line. It's such a fine line, and we definitely don't want some like national geographic type exploration of the work. I'll just say quickly you have to understand your own whiteness and understand that if you truly understand hip-hop, then you know that you can't hide from yourself to authentically engage in this work. That the more authentic you are presenting yourself, even if you look and sound nothing like hip-hop it is hip-hop if it is authentic.

So, I don't know if that answers it, it's a hard thing to crack, and I love talking about it cause I will say that this is not a topic that I talk about regularly as a scholar out loud. I think about a lot of this stuff in isolation, Edmund and I have talked briefly about this at points, but like, you know, what would it look like for scholars to really come together and develop an approach to getting folks comfortable, understanding the culture in more, in more deep ways.

A lack of interrogation of whiteness in the implementation of hip-hop pedagogy and research can contribute to a replication of the same systemic inequities that hip-hop seeks to eradicate. Therefore, not interrogating whiteness and your overall positionality as it relates to hip-hop culture is accepting a default to the status quo of society and the institution of education, which is a position of whiteness. Additionally, authenticity is essential in this process for Dr. Levy. Authenticity and a broader understanding of self have always been imperative in hip-hop; so imperative, in fact, that one of the elements of hip-hop is knowledge of self. Knowledge of self "encourages participants of hip-hop culture to be aware of who they are, be authentic to themselves, and be confident in themselves to make positive social-political change for their communities" (Adjapong, 2017, p.16). Therefore, "for the hip-hop generation, engagement in any element of hip-hop without knowledge of self-connotes inauthenticity….engaging in rap without knowledge of self is not an authentic representation of hip-hop culture" (Adjapong & Levy, 2020, p.4). Similarly, Adjapong & Levy (2020) argue that "engaging in hip-hop scholarship without knowledge of self is an inauthentic representation" of hip-hop education (p. 4). This understanding of knowledge of self must include an understanding of one's positionality and how that positionality intersects with the structures, systems, policies, and practices they engage with. This knowledge of self must also include a historical understanding of the structures, systems, policies, and practices that individuals operate within.

Edmund:	I agree with you in the sense that the work has never been to convert people to become like participants of the culture, right? And I think you acknowledge that it's more so like, "Yo, I just want you to value my culture." And if people see the value in it, then they might see the necessity to leverage it in spaces to support youth. Nobody's going to leverage hip-hop in any space, inside or outside the academy, if they don't see their value in it. So I agree. I think that might be the first step.
Dr. Ian Levy:	Yeah. And I think what's frustrating to me is the people who feel like they don't understand hip-hop or can't do it, you know? But like there are a million cultures and subcultures of other things that people don't ask this question about.
Edmund:	Yeah. I attribute that to hip-hop and its symbiotic relationship with Blackness. Like, you know, people are, you know, that's Black culture.
Dr. Ian Levy:	It's just anti-Blackness, that's what it comes down to.
Edmund:	And I think that's the thing that we don't recognize that it's through the guise of hip-hop. It's not just hip-hop because people see hip-hop as Blackness. So in some way, when you're like, "Yo, we want you to leverage hip-hop in spaces." What people really hear is, "Yo, we want you to leverage Blackness in spaces." Which is true, we do want that.
Dr. Ian Levy:	Yeah, yeah, yeah.
Edmund:	But I think that's where the apprehension comes, where people are like, "Well, I'm not versed in Black culture." And then there's this apprehension of wanting to engage, and there's fear around doing things wrong.

As Dr. Levy and Edmund point out, hip-hop has always been synonymous with Blackness and Black culture. Essential in understanding why hip-hop is such an integral aspect of Black culture is first understanding that *hip-hop is a culture* with distinct cultural practices and representations. To this end, hip-hop is sometimes regarded as a Black subculture (Clay, 2003). In order to fully understand the cultural practices and representations in hip-hop culture, there has to be an understanding of the society, culture, and conditions that created the cultural production and consumption (Kibona Clark, 2018;

Ingram, 2010). Central to the practices and representations of hip-hop are Black youth because Black youth are often at the forefront of innovation in hip-hop (Emdin et al., 2016). The perspectives of Black youth and the way they perceive and enact hip-hop are important because,

> "truth and reality are not neutral but constructed. As a form of cultural representation, hip-hop is no different. The artists themselves decide what is relevant and what realities they want to construct. Whatever is produced—be it music, a graffiti tag, a graphic design on a t-shirt, or a film—the cultural production encompasses the ideologies and backgrounds of the artist(s)" (Kibona Clark, 2018, p. 2).

Therefore, to understand hip-hop as Black culture is to understand Black youth. Further, research has demonstrated that Black youth see engagement in hip-hop culture as a Black subculture and ultimately utilize engagement in hip-hop as a measure of Blackness (Clay, 2003). Specifically, Black youth privilege the performance of hip-hop identity through engagement in hip-hop music, gestures, language, and fashion (Clay, 2003). Similarly, hip-hop has been used by Black southerners as a conduit of Black identity; specifically, Black southern youth have used hip-hop as a way to construct a contemporary southern Black identity that expands understanding of what it means to be Black in the south (Bradley, 2021). Hip-Hop has had the ability to write stories from personal experiences that spoke to the Black experience (Clay, 2003; Rose, 1994). This centering of lyrical storytelling rooted in the reality of the Black experience assisted in hip-hop being deemed "the very blackest culture" (Gilroy, 1997, p. 85).

Edmund: The last question, if you could radically dream about the future of the field of hip-hop and education, what would you envision? Like what would you want to see?

Dr. Ian Levy: I want to see a full school that uses hip-hop across everything. I don't even know a school that has two hip-hop educators. It's either like, there's a cool Science Genius program running here, you know. I've done some counseling work at my school, but hip-hop work usually exists in isolation in school buildings, so there's only one entry point for hip-hop. I'd love to see there be multiple entry points through all content areas and then through all other structures, right through school support services like counseling. What would it look like for like educational leaders for hip-hop to be imbued in leadership? And just the way that the school is structured and defined. I would love to see that, and that would then allow really robust and cool intervention work to happen. When the entire school is engaging in the work, you can really start looking at things you can do. I'm a researcher at heart, so that you can do longitudinal studies. What does it look like for a year, you know, a ninth-grade class to enter a hip-hop based high school And then study what happens across that four years developmentally? How do you track knowledge of self and, and this thing, these inherent those sensibilities that we were talking about, how do you see those develop and measure them and, and report on them? So that folks know like, yo like, look like, look at like the beautiful things that happen when the entire system is built, the entire ecosystem is built and rooted in hip-hop. And so I guess my dream is like just the hip-hop, like schools and ecosystems and because it's, it's too frustrating in isolation when you're that one educator in a building trying to do the work, um, and I, you know, that's necessary for now of course, but, but I'd love to see that change.

Dr. Levy's radical dream for the future of the field of hip-hop and education is to see whole school ecosystems and communities utilize hip-hop as a philosophy in regard to decision-making and practice, which will allow for longitudinal and more rigorous research studies to be conducted on the impact, benefits and challenges of hip-hop and education practices. In educational leadership, Mountain (2019) discusses an approach to hip-hop principalship that is grounded in five tenets, including authenticity, speaking truth to power, challenging the status quo, community accountability, and creativity and autonomy. In relation to pedagogy, scholars have explored the use of hip-hop across multiple content areas such as science (Adjapong, 2017, 2019; Adjapong & Emdin, 2015; Emdin, 2010), English (Kelly, 2013; Lyiscott, 2017), civic engagement (Love, 2014; Schupp, 2019), math (Amidon, 2013; Tillman, 2016), and the arts (Kruse, 2016). There have also been studies that explored hip-hop informed out-of-school programming, such as the Science Genius Program (Adjapong, 2019), Queens Public Library Hip-Hop Initiatives, and True Skool in Milwaukee, to name a few. While there is a plethora of work that leverages the beauty and nuance of hip-hop within educational spaces, it is very rare to see one school building/community that is holistically informed by hip-hop. Hip-Hop in education praxis too often occurs in siloes, which can limit and slow progress. As we are able to imagine radically dream about new schools and educational spaces, we should collectively push for these spaces to authentically incorporate hip-hop into various spaces within the community, such as leadership, pedagogy, culture, community partnership, etc., to better understand the relationship between the use of hip-hop within various educational context.

To learn more about Dr. Ian Levy's research and scholarship, check out the following:

- Levy, I. P., & Keum, B. T. (2022). Supporting school counselor's multicultural self-efficacy development through Hip Hop based coursework. *Journal of Poetry Therapy*, 1–21. https://doi.org/10.1080/08893675.2022.2131473.
- Adjapong, E., & Levy, I. (2021). Hip-Hop can heal: Addressing mental health through hip-hop in the urban classroom. *The New Educator*, 17(3), 242–263. https://doi.org/10.1080/1547688X.2020.1849884.
- Levy, I. (2021). *Hip-Hop and spoken word therapy in school counseling: Developing culturally responsive approaches*. Routledge.
- Levy, I. P., & Adjapong, E. S. (2020). Toward culturally competent school counseling environments: Hip-Hop studio construction. *Professional Counselor*, 10(2), 266–284.

References

Adjapong, E. (2019). Towards a practice of emancipation in urban schools: A look at student experiences through the science genius battles program. *Journal of Ethnic and Cultural Studies*, 6(1), 15–27. https://doi.org/10.29333/ejecs/136.

Adjapong, E., & Allen, K. R. (2023). For White folks who teach hip-hop—and the rest of Ya'll, too: Interrogating the positionality of hip-hop educators and researchers. *Equity & Excellence in Education*, 1–14.

Adjapong, E. S. (2017). Bridging theory and practice in the urban science classroom: A framework for hip-hop pedagogy in STEM. *Critical Education*, 8, 15.

Adjapong, E. S., & Emdin, C. (2015). Rethinking pedagogy in urban spaces: Implementing hip-hop pedagogy in the urban science classroom. *Journal of Urban Learning, Teaching, and Research*, 11, 66–77.

Amidon, J. (2013). Teaching mathematics as agape: Responding to oppression with unconditional love. *Journal of Urban Mathematics Education*, 6(1), 19–27.

Bradley, R. (2021). *Chronicling Stankonia: The rise of the hip-hop south*. The University of North Carolina Press.

Chang, J. (2007). *Can't stop won't stop: A history of the hip-hop generation*. St. Martin's Press.

Clay, A. (2003). Keepin' it real: Black youth, hip-hop culture, and Black identity. *The American Behavioral Scientist*, 46(10), 1346–1358. https://doi.org/10.1177/0002764203046010005.

Cummings, J. R., & Druss, B. G. (2011). Racial/ethnic differences in mental health service use among adolescents with major depression. *Journal of the American Academy of Child & Adolescent Psychiatry*, 50, 160–170. http://dx.doi.org/10.1016/j.jaac.2010.11.004.

Emdin, C. (2010). Affiliation and alienation: Hip-Hop, rap, and urban science education. *Journal of Curriculum Studies*, *42*(1), 1–25. https://doi.org/10.1080/00220270903161118.

Emdin, C., Adjapong, E., & Levy, I. (2016). Hip-hop based interventions as pedagogy/therapy in STEM: A model from urban science education. *Journal for Multicultural Education*, *10*(3), 307-321.

Gilroy, P. (1997). "After the love has gone": Bio-politics and etho-poetics in the Black public sphere. In A. McRobbie (Ed.), *Back to reality? Social experience and cultural studies* (pp. 83–115). Manchester, UK: Manchester University Press.

Ingram, B. (2010). Music. In M. Ryan, B. Ingram & H. Musiol (Eds.), *Cultural studies: A practical introduction* (pp. 105–121). Malden, MA: Wiley-Blackwell.

Kelly, L. L. (2013). Hip-Hop literature: The politics, poetics, and power of hip-hop in the English classroom. *English Journal*, *102*(5), 51–56.

Kibona Clark, M. (2018). *Hip-Hop in Africa: Prophets of the city and dustyfoot philosophers*. Ohio University Press.

Kruse, A. J. (2016). Toward hip-hop pedagogies for music education. *International Journal of Music Education*, *34*(2), 247–260.

Levy, I. P. (2020). "Real Recognize Real": Hip-Hop spoken word therapy and humanistic practice. *The Journal of Humanistic Counseling*, *59*(1), 38–53.

Love, B. L. (2014). Urban storytelling: How storyboarding, moviemaking, and hip-hop-based education can promote Students' critical voice. *English Journal*, *103*(5), 53–58.

Lyiscott, J. (2017). Racial identity and liberation literacies in the classroom. *English Journal*, *106*(4), 47–53.

Mountain, B. A. (2019). The reflective principal: Turning the tables. *Principal*, *98*(4), 50–51.

Rose, T. (1994). *Black noise: Rap music and Black culture in contemporary America*. Wesleyan University Press.

Schupp, K. (2019). Dance competition culture and commercial dance: Intertwined aesthetics, values, and practices. *Journal of Dance Education*, *19*(2), 58–67.

Tillman, D. A. (2016). Learning from the College Dropout: Depictions of numeracy and mathematics within hip-hop music. *Journal of Mathematics Education*, *9*, 53–71.

· 4 ·

TOWARDS A CRITICAL CENTERING OF YOUTH PERSPECTIVES ON HIP-HOP EDUCATION: KEEPING IT REAL WITH DAVID STOVALL

Dr. Stovall's work utilizes critical race theory and critical race practices to understand the relationship between race, place, and school. Specifically, Dr. Stovall's work encourages individuals to move beyond academic texts to make sense of how youth culture and experiences influence education. For Dr. Stovall, hip-hop is important in his practice because of how integral youth has been and continues to be in the formation and perpetuation of hip-hop.

Edmund:	You talk a lot about the connections between schools and youth culture. How do you align yourself with hip-hop and your work? What's the connection between yourself, your identity and hip-hop, and your work?
Dr. David Stovall:	As someone who tries to be supportive of the culture, I understand it as the creation of young people, right? And it was the creation of young people in response in many ways to uneven urban development/gentrification. So, I always think about hip-hop as an intentional response to a city's strategy that tried to push them out. And young people create ways by which to build an understanding of each other and themselves through places where they can gather and express themselves through the arts.
Edmund:	That's dope. As a scholar, what motivates you? You've touched on why hip-hop, motivates you to contribute to work in hip-hop and education.

Dr. David Stovall: I think of it as a responsibility. Because this was the way in which young people were communicating. So, a lot of times, as I got older and still working with young folks, I considered what it means to be responsible for the ways that young folks communicate with each other. As well, what do young folks understand as relevant and necessary in their world? And can hip-hop now provide that particular understanding or that communicative form that folks can understand because as folks get older, they try to distance themselves from young people. And a lot of times, what I noticed, particularly as being a professor, people miss the point a lot. And one of the things that academia does is to bastardize everything that it does not understand. So, for me, I always felt that I was trying to engage in an attempt to really think about what it means to move differently. So that was always in my perspective in terms of what I was trying to do in relationship to hip-hop.

Dr. Stovall recognizes hip-hop as a culture created by youth in response to systemic oppression, including urban development and gentrification, particularly within inner cities, which resulted in the displacement of community members who suffered the decisions of politicians and those in power. Amid experiencing oppressive practices and strategies, youth have leveraged hip-hop as a way to heal, and respond to the oppression faced within their very own communities. Hip-Hop provides an opportunity for youth to make sense of their own experiences and learn about the experiences and realities of those within their communities. This response to oppression can be conceptualized as a form of *collective agency*. *Collective agency* involves the understanding that social actors have the ability to create and enact behavioral options necessary to affect their political future (White, 2019). Further, theories around collective agency contend that how individuals "conceptualize their own agency affects their beliefs about whether they can influence the course of events in their own lives" (White, p. 7, 2019). To this end, hip-hop can be positioned as a social and behavioral response to oppression that facilitated understanding of individuals' positions in society. This collective meaning making is imperative for social and political liberation. In his research on youth culture and hip-hop, Dr. Stovall recognized that adults often try to distance themselves from youth—as opposed to centering youth—and as a result, misunderstand the needs and realities of youth. In consequence, academia and education writ large often misappropriate hip-hop culture and divorces it from the roots of collective agency, meaning making, and liberation.

Edmund: Considering the field of hip-hop in education right now—thinking of the work that's come out over the last 10–15 years or so—what are your overall thoughts on the field of hip-hop and education?

Dr. David Stovall: Yeah, I like when folks are interrogating hip-hop as culture, but also, I am deeply concerned and worried because I'm always concerned about something being co-opted. I'm always concerned about something being fad-ish.

Edmund: Yeah, that's real. You talked about your fear around academia bastardizing and fetishizing things. So in relation to that, what challenges might persist in the field of hip-hop and education?

Dr. David Stovall: I think one of the challenges is just because you listen to hip-hop does not mean that you know hip-hop. I think that's a really important thing to say. And just because you study hip-hop culture doesn't necessarily mean that you understand it. You all probably saw this work that just got pulled by this professor out of Azusa Pacific University called *Bad and Bougie: Toward a Trap Feminist Theology*. So, she's using the Migos song [Bad and Bougie] and talking about trap Queens from the perspective of a White woman from the suburbs—*you cannot do that shit*. I'm not trying to stand as a gatekeeper, but you can't do that with any responsibility or integrity to a community that you say you care about. Like that doesn't make sense. So now, what does it mean to do your work with some integrity and some fidelity to the people who are immersed in that [hip-hop] culture? So, the claim around, you're interested in hip-hop, and it intrigues you and now that's why you study it doesn't work for me. It's really around how do you understand the work that young people have engaged to create and resist? And when you start to do that with some integrity, I feel like the work reads differently. I feel like the work sounds different. And I think that it allows people to engage in it [authentically]. So, for me, the worry is when people just think that hip-hop is this thing to be studied, it's further objectified. Now that is not to be dismissive of how hip-hop has become commodified in the world of late-stage capitalism. But when I think about it as culture, I'm deeply concerned that people just kind of make this claim that they're interested in the culture, that they like the music, and now this is what necessarily makes them an expert. The claim to expertise by academics in and of itself is a colonial project. And one that's rooted in a relative assumption of what's rational, according to European standards. So, for me, I'm always leery of folks who have no real connection to hip-hop, other than listening to the music and liking it.

Like many hip-hop scholars, Dr. Stovall is concerned with hip-hop culture being co-opted or misappropriated by academics, educators and outsiders of the culture who find themselves interrogating the culture. Stovall highlights that *"just because you listen to hip-hop does not mean that you know hip-hop."* Because you are a consumer of hip-hop music, does not qualify you to be an expert on hip-hop culture. Hip-Hop culture is so complex and nuanced that in order to identify as an expert, in our opinion, requires an individual to be proximal to youth in inner-city communities and to repeatedly co-interrogating their realities and understand how young people make sense of their realities. But can anyone truly be an expert of hip-hop a forever evolving culture that exist slightly different in various context?

One challenge of engaging in hip-hop education research is fear of the misappropriation of the culture. The Cambridge Dictionary (n.d.) defines cultural appropriation as "the act of taking or using things from a culture that is not your own, especially without showing that you understand or respect this culture." It's important to recognize that to understand and respect hip-hop culture requires the researcher and educator to decenter themselves and be proximal to youth who are creating and innovating hip-hop culture. You don't get a pass on critically reflecting on your identity just because of your interest of hip-hop culture. While we may have good intentions of leveraging hip-hop in educational spaces, it's more important to deeply understand the possible impact (negative and/or positive) that our scholarship and pedagogy may have on youth and communities. Regardless of the intention, without a deep interrogation of self, we risk misappropriating hip-hop culture because "Black culture is intentionally being made palatable to a White audience, with the goal of making a profit" (Cherid, 2021, p. 360).

Further, Dr. Stovall is concerned with hip-hop centered research in academic spaces being a fad, a interest that is very popular for a short period of time. When hip-hop was birthed during the 1970s society thought that the innovation, creativity, and resilience that contributed to the creation of hip-hop culture would not be long lived. During the 1970s and 1980s many believed that hip-hop would be a fad, but over the last five decades hip-hop culture has proven to be resilient and has served as the backdrop to pivotal moments in Black history such as Los Angeles riots of 1992, the 2008 presidential election of Barack Obama, the Black Lives Matter protest of 2020 to name a few. Dr. Stovall's fear of hip-hop centered research in academic spaces becoming a fad comes from researchers who may not fully understand the complexities, nuance and communities that contribute to hip-hop culture offering superficial and basic interpretations of hip-hop that do not necessarily extend the knowledge in the field. As educators and scholars, we must continue to interrogate hip-hop culture to understand the many benefits as well as critique and offer plausible solutions to the challenges of the culture that we observe. We must also advocate for the history of hip-hop to be taught in schools so that young people are aware of the brilliance, innovation and resilience that birthed hip-hop culture and recognize that hip-hop is not solely a genre of music, but a culture that is worth a deep interrogation and exploration.

Edmund: That's real. I get that. We recognize that too. Kelly and I, we just wrote a paper focused on white folks in particular, but all educators, including Black folks that provides a framework on interrogating their positionality as it relates to hip-hop culture. Before anyone engages in hip-hop and education research or practice or scholarship there needs to be a deep dive into who they are and who they are in relationship to Black culture and hip-hop culture.

Dr. David Stovall: Exactly. You have to be able to do inward facing work. That is the thing, that's the key in terms of being responsible to your work, it has to be inward facing.

Because of the dangers of co-option, Dr. Stovall encourages educators to examine their positionality in relation to hip-hop. In our article, *For White Folks Who Teach Hip-Hop…and the Rest of Ya'll Too: Interrogating the Positionality of Hip-Hop Educators and Researchers*, we encourage and provide a practical framework for educators and researchers to interrogate their positionality as it relates to hip-hop culture and the Black and Brown communities who created and continue to innovate the culture (Adjapong & Allen, 2023). We argue that in order for educators to engage in authentic and effective hip-hop and education research and/or praxis, there must be an interrogation positionality (including racial identity), and how this positionality relates to and interacts with institutions, systems, and the hip-hop populations the individual is engaged with. We believe that it is imperative that hip-hop educators and researchers interrogate their positionality in relation to hip-hop populations as it relates to their teaching, learning, and research context while centering on Black voices, experiences, and realities. To support hip-hop educators and researchers in understanding how to interrogate their positionality as it relates to hip-hop populations, we draw from Milner's (2007) Framework of Researcher Racial and Cultural Position, which provides a platform for educators and researchers to process racial and cultural awareness, consciousness, and positionality and includes the following tenets: researching the self, researching the self in relation to others, engaged reflection and representation, and shifting from self to system.

Edmund:	We know that you know you conducted research in social studies classrooms around social studies curriculum. In one of your articles, you talked about lyrics and utilizing hip-hop lyrics in the social studies curriculum. Can you talk a little bit about that work? I think it's powerful in terms of thinking about the practical approaches that teachers can leverage in their classroom. In your perspective, what's the power of leveraging lyrics as curriculum or as hip-hop curriculum? And what are some examples of how you have seen teachers grapple, participate, and engage in this type of work and curriculum?
Dr. David Stovall:	Yeah. You know, lyrics are context, right? Lyrics provide context and provide a pathway to inquiry. So when people are able to think about what's being expressed, it's really different when you see it in text form…and I think as I stated, I was listening to what my students were listening to. And then I was trying to contrast it to kind of the stuff that I was listening to for them to ask the questions around where they saw the similarities and differences… I was just talking to an English teacher last summer and she was like, "You know, if they are rocking with Little Baby, I got to get on Lil Baby. If they listening to Durk, I got to listen to Durk." But what she was telling me was she has to take the Lil Dirk, King Von and all of those spaces and really kind of get to not just the trap lyrics, but to ask themselves "what are they saying about everyday struggle"? So here in the Chi, there's a guy who's come on the scene and gotten some notoriety nationally. He used to be called Lil Herb, but now everybody knows him as G Herbo. And Herbo is really community minded. He's from a particular neighborhood that is kind of isolated and he's always been intentional about saying, "Okay, how can I make sure that young folks are seeing not only what's possible, but also telling their truth?" So I think that's really important in terms of understanding that expression. And that's what Black folks, Puerto Ricans, Filipino folks who have really been embracing and engaging the culture have really kind of set themselves up to do, right? Because it's a form of expression to now speak back in many ways to white supremacy and say, "your norms are not my norms and I'm willing to do something different now." Of course, late-stage capitalism complicates a lot of that. And we do get hyper objectified lyrics, especially when you talk about misogyny, right? But at the same time now, how are we able to use that to decipher how young folks are seeing their world, not as an academic exercise, but to say, if this is how you're

	understanding your world now, what are ways that we can work—could jointly get together to work—to shift our realities? I think that's a really important piece. So, I'm seeing folks who are using lyrics as context, right? It's a context, it's a window into a moment and it's a way to engage analysis, right. In terms of really kind of thinking about our work differently.
Edmund:	That's dope.
Kelly:	That's dope. And, you know as I'm listening to you talk, I'm like, "YES." And I wonder how you respond to teachers, admins—whoever you may be working with—that say, "No, I get that the kids like King Von. I get like, they like G. Herbo. But I'm not bringing that 'trap stuff' into my classroom" because they don't necessarily see the connection to—you know, you were just saying the community mindedness and those types of things? How do you respond to people who are like, "No, if I'm going to bring hip-hop in, it's going to be on my terms and it's going to be the music that I like." How do you respond to that?
Dr. David Stovall:	Right. And thank you for that question. I tell folks they're dead from the start. I mean, if you not willing to engage where young folks are, you won't be able to move the needle. I mean that's just a basic thing. And the first thing is that inward facing work. You have to say to yourself, "Okay, my young folks are into different stuff. I need to understand that." If I'm talking about reaching them in a place like school, that was never meant to do right by them in the first place, then I have to flip that understanding. I got to do something different. I mean in the early days—this is going to sound funny to y'all—you know, but I wasn't necessarily checking for Luda. And my young bloods were Ludicrous deep. And I'm like, "All right, look, I need to fuck with that." Just off top. Because if I don't then I'm just reifying that alienation. I'm just making it for the stuff that I like. You know, you not going to come into a class where folks may be into Neo Soul playing Lionel Richie. That's not going to work. I mean we just have to be honest about that. And I think you can say to teachers that they have to start in a particular way. Now, you can bring different stuff in and ask different questions. Hip-Hop was always a transition for me to really kind of talk about jazz, to talk about blues, to talk about rock. So it was an entry point to engage different music. So now those teachers who are resistant, they have to think about how they're going to bring in what their young folks feel is relevant. And now transition that to learn about other styles, moments, history. This is the pathway to really understand social context through music. The thing I would tell folks is that if they not willing to do that, it just won't make sense. And that's just being honest with ourselves

	and being very clear about the necessity of inward facing work. We just have to do that. You know here in Chicago when people talk about drill music or what have you, the cat who invented the term lives right around the corner from me, King Louie. And King Louie was valedictorian of his high school class. A good dude, solid dude. And when he talks about drill, one of the things that he was very honest about is a lot of the drill music that you hear is really about personal frustration. So, you got to be able to engage that—not stay at that point—but start at that point so that you know what it is when you look at the work. So don't worry about those teachers who are resistant. You can tell 'em they need to do something different, and young folks are going to show you real quick what does not work.
Edmund:	That's real.

Dr. Stovall's assertion that educators must recognize, honor, and sustain students' hip-hop identities in the classroom is an embodiment of conscientization. Conscientization posits that individuals and communities develop a critical understanding of their social reality through reflection and subsequent action (Freire, 2012). A key part of this reflection is an acknowledgment and examination of oppression. Dr. Stovall's discussion of trap music demonstrates how misunderstood experiences of individuals in the hood are. While topics of physical violence and drug use may not be considered suitable topics for classroom consumption by predominantly white educators who have not lived in, experienced, and/or critically reflected on the experiences by individuals living in the hood, these topics are everyday experiences of oppression for youth in the hood. If we are to imagine a liberatory education for youth from the hood, we must engage in a critical examination of the oppressive experiences outlined in hip-hop music. To this end Freire contends,

> "we must never merely discourse on the present situation, must never provide the people with programs which have little or nothing to do with their own preoccupations, doubts, hopes, and fears—programs which at times in fact increase the fears of the oppressed consciousness. It is not our role to speak to the people about our own view of the world, nor to attempt to impose that view on them, but rather to dialogue with the people about their view and ours. We must realize that their view of the world, manifested variously in their action, reflects their situation in the world. Educational and political actions which is not critically aware of the situation runs the risk either of "banking" or of preaching in the desert" (Freire, 2012, p. 96).

Rejecting trap music because the topics are not considered suitable, and instead bringing in narratives that feel suitable to the educator, is a marginalizing and oppressive act. A critical part of engaging in this level of social awareness includes a critical reflection of self. Therefore, Dr. Stovall encourages educators to engage in critical reflection about their own perceptions of hip-hop.

Edmund: I know a lot of your work is focused on critical race theory, but a majority of your research has been centered on social justice. How can all educators from K-20 that you engage in your research? How can educators within all these contexts leverage, and be critical of social justice, issues of social justice?

Dr. David Stovall: Yeah. I mean, I think this thing around really thinking about what are these justice conditions, right? If we understand and know that there are spaces that people have determined are not working, and now they say, well, justice is whatever. We have determined what the justice condition is, because we have experienced injustice. Now that's where our conversation goes. Because a lot of times, this kind of social justice rhetoric, has been completely co-opted.

Yeah. So now it's really around, okay. What does that mean in real time for communities? What is the injustice that people are trying to address? So, as you all framed it, right, what is that freedom dream? How are we connected to it? And what are we trying to do to build it and not to take it beyond the rhetorical, right? Not to take it as just language, but to really kind of check what Robin D.G. Kelley is saying about a freedom dream. It's what are you willing to build knowing that these other things are not working. So education is that process to build those things, because these other things are not working.

I feel like I learn a lot from prison abolitionists who say, look, you know, and we know that prisons nor police stop crime. So now if I know that to be true, here's what I'm willing to do differently. I think this is that moment. We're in a moment where we can actually begin to talk about that in serious ways, but also ways that are connected to young folks who are demanding justice conditions.

Kelly: If you could radically dream about the future of hip-hop and education what would you envision?

Dr. David Stovall: Yeah, a great question. I think for me, I just want to really have spaces where young people can create and think on their own terms, but also connect that to their interests and then really think about how are we learning, what are we learning? Also, to co-collaborate with students on that. So, it's not just the three of us as appointed PhDs, sitting around saying, okay, here's what we can do, blah, blah, blah. But instead saying, all right, well, let's, let's workshop this with a group of young folks, let's get into a classroom and rock with a group of young folks and then have them evaluate our stuff as opposed to whatever walkthrough that the school district does or whatever, you know, the bullshit that they put forward. But what does it mean to really kind of put your stuff on "front street", as the elders say. So, this thing around really being intentional about that and really kind of rethinking the radical dream as rethinking how we create curriculum and how we engage young folks. Because there are teachers who have done this for time and memorial, but we've never given them their roses. We've never recognized them. And I think in our recognition of them, we have to use those strategies in ways that allow us to share what we are doing with each other.

When engaging in work, practice and scholarship focused on social justice, it's important to center the voices and experiences of groups who have faced injustice. Centering the voices of those who have experienced injustice provides an opportunity to support in empowering these groups and identifying practical solutions to making shifts within systems, policies and practices that contribute to the injustice. Dr. Stovall's radical dream is that education is the process that supports justice. Contexts of education, such as schools and community organizations have the ability to bring together communities to engage in dialogue to identify challenges contributing to injustice and to identify solutions, and finally act towards enacting liberatory solutions. Dr. Stovall's radical dream can be actualized if we move away from the "banking" concept of education, which Freire (2012) describes students as depositories and teachers as depositors of content, attitudes, and practices that mirror oppressive societies. The "banking" concept of education perpetuates a cycle of oppression within historically marginalized communities and does not support young people in identifying solutions to injustices faced within the community. Further, Freire (2012) demonstrates that we must engage in dialogue to identify and name problems and challenges that exist and impact our communities. Freire (2012) posits, "I engage in dialogue not necessarily because I like the other person. I engage in dialogue because I recognize the social and not merely the individualistic character of the process of knowing" (pg. 10). When engaging in dialogue, the goal is not consensus, rather to support the process of knowing as means towards liberation. Because of this, dialogue must not be a situation where some name on behalf of others. Dialogue is an act of creation between those in power and those who have experienced injustice with the goal of the world for the liberation of humankind. Dr. Stovall suggests that all scholars and educators engaging in justice work must center youth and those directly impacted. There can no longer be contexts where *only* scholars and educators, who have no connection to communities, are sitting around a table seeking solutions to injustice. We must reconsider how we engage youth in schools and focus on empowering their voices through curriculum and content. Finally, if we are engaged in hip-hop centered practices, we must center the voices of historically marginalized groups to gain an authentic perspective of the daily challenges and injustices that contribute to one's experiences; this is the true essence of hip-hop, as hip-hop culture was created for the liberation of historically marginalized communities.

To learn more about Dr. David Stovall's research and scholarship, check out the following:

- Stovall, D. (2006). We can relate: Hip-Hop culture, critical pedagogy, and the secondary classroom. *Urban Education, 41*(6), 585–602.
- Stovall, D. (2016). *Born out of struggle: Critical race theory, school creation and the politics of interruption.* Albany: SUNY Press.
- Stovall, D. (2022). The enemy said we will not make it home: Critical race theory, educational foundations and the fight against precarity. *Educational Studies, 58*(4), 421–434.

References

Adjapong, E., & Allen, K. R. (2023). For White folks who teach hip-hop—and the rest of Ya'll, too: Interrogating the positionality of hip-hop educators and researchers. *Equity & Excellence in Education,* 1–14.

Freire, P. (2012). *Pedagogy of the oppressed.* Rowman & Littlefield.

White, M. M. (2019). *Freedom farmers: Agricultural resistance and the Black freedom movement.* Chapel Hill: The University of North Carolina Press.

· 5 ·

CULTIVATING INTERSECTIONAL PERSPECTIVES OF HIP-HOP EDUCATION: KEEPING IT REAL WITH MARCELLA RUNELL HALL

Dr. Marcella Runell Hall is the Vice President for Student Life and Dean of Students at Mount Holyoke College, where she also serves as a lecturer of religion. Dr. Runell Hall is best known for her work and research in social justice education and hip-hop education curriculum development. Dr. Runell Hall, in collaboration with Martha Diaz, designed *The Hip-Hop Education Guidebook: Volume 1*, a curricular resource that illustrates the creativity of hip-hop music and culture with the goal of making schools and classrooms more engaging.

Edmund: Can you explain how you identify yourself as a scholar and what groups you consider, primarily, in your research?

Dr. Runell Hall: My background started in social work and what was then women's studies, then I transitioned into higher education administration and Africana studies at NYU, and then I moved into social justice education for my graduate work. So I'm interdisciplinary, but for social identity and personal identity, I would first start by saying that my parents were Irish, so I identify as Irish, using racial constructs I am white. I was raised working class, middle-class, now I'm solidly middle-class, you know, upper middle class, in some regards because of education and other things. I am an able-bodied heterosexual, and these are not important things that, that you all need to be considering, but just so you know, I come with a certain level of privilege to the conversation in terms of social constructs in the US. That's obviously relevant.

Then how did I come into hip-hop for my choice of scholarship? I was born in Washington, DC, and grew up in the Northeast. Hip-Hop was a big part of my youth. So my whole youth middle school, elementary school, and high school were about hip-hop, and it was about pop culture, and it was about relationships and a lot of tense interactions around race and pop culture. There was a lot going on, but there was also this desire to find bridges and to be able to connect. Hip-Hop, for me, was that way of connection—it was social capital. When I moved in and out of different spaces, it was a way to share common interests. Most importantly, it was a way to understand the world. Cause I felt like the adults, the grownups, weren't really explaining a lot about why things were the way they were. I saw the injustice with my friends regarding racism and classism, incarceration, and all the different pieces of what was going on in the late 80s and early 90s. I didn't have a lot of insight into why. I felt like hip-hop was the place where I started to be able to get answers, like to some of the systems, some of the history, some of the connections. And so that was like a big core part of who I was as a young person. When I got to college, and I was majoring in social work and doing all the things, I was really action-oriented about—I thought about how I can make a difference. How can I show up? But hip-hop was still personal, and it was private. It was like in my social space, it was not in my scholarly space. I didn't even know that was possible until I got to NYU. There I met Robin Kelly and Trisha Rose and Nelson George, and all these people. I was like, wait, what? You can actually study this. Like, you could take classes with people who will help you make meaning of this. It was the greatest discovery of my entire academic life.

Edmund: What motivates you to contribute to work on hip-hop education?

Dr. Runell Hall: Early on, when I was connecting with Martha Diaz, who I co-wrote the hip-hop education guidebook with, she and I were very upfront with each other. I said, "I don't ever wanna be the face of this." I'm not trying to come in and control any of this or take it over. But if I can be useful in my identities and my position, then please use me, like put me to work. Let me be useful because the reality is no matter how you look at it, there's still a disproportionate amount of K-12 teachers who are white women. So one of the things that I wanted to be helpful in doing was to say, "You don't get a pass out of this because you don't think that this is your culture." It doesn't have to be your culture, right?

> I always used the example because David Kirkland was so good about saying how Shakespeare wasn't anybody's culture, but people learned it, right? I mean, way back in the day, it was the people's culture. But I mean not now. Teachers learn how to teach Shakespeare without question whether or not that is their culture, and so the thing for me was how can I be useful in saying this is not just an optional thing. It is your responsibility to learn and to take this seriously. There are enough resources out there now, enough research and enough access points through curriculum and through all the different teaching artists and the ways that we have taken all of this and created these avenues for teachers. There's no excuse. So that was it for me. Just trying to listen to people that I trusted and mentors that I had, who were saying, we actually need you. And here's how we need you to show up. That authenticity in my heart and my spirit around it was in alignment. But I really wanted to be as useful as possible.

As Dr. Runell Hall discusses, the responsibility to engage in work around hip-hop education cannot solely be on teachers, scholars, and community members of color. In academia, this disparate burden is well documented. Many faculty of color bear the onus of educating their white counterparts about the deleterious effects of racism and whiteness in education policy and practice (Gibson, 2019; Laura, 2019). For faculty of color, the burden of unveiling institutional racism and white patriarchy can lead to racial battle fatigue and is often undervalued and uncompensated by tenure review boards and white colleagues (Bridget & Winkle-Wagner, 2017; Croom, 2017; Garrison-Wade et al., 2012; Gibson et al., 2017; Haynes et al., 2020; Levin et al., 2015, Tanner, 2019). To continue to place the burden of this work on individuals of color is a perpetuation and intensification of the racialized labor burden of individuals of color in education.

Beyond the racialized labor burden, the very aim of hip-hop education demands the involvement of all individuals invested in education. One of the main recurring arguments for the use of hip-hop education is mostly the same—to address concerns regarding the lack of culturally responsive approaches in teaching and learning and encourage students to have a deeper connection with their communities and critically interrogate systems and structures that directly impact them (Adjapong, 2017; Pechauer, 2009). At the time of its founding, hip-hop was rooted in the disruption of whiteness and the oppression it produces for communities of color (Chang, 2007; Rose, 1994). While the commercialization of hip-hop has at times attempted to remove hip-hop from these roots (Blair, 2004), if we are to honor the roots of hip-hop, then we must acknowledge that at its core, hip-hop in education is founded in the disruption of whiteness. Runell and Diaz (2007) explain that hip-hop education is a "layered approach founded on social justice education and embedded in hip-hop culture" (p. 15). Central to implementing hip-hop education is an understanding of the layers of oppression that exist in society and the belief that the social identities of students, teachers, and community members matter (Runell & Diaz, 2007). Is this work solely relegated to teachers, scholars, and community members of color? If this is work only to be undertaken by individuals of color, what, then, are the goals and purpose of white people in education? As Love (2019) explains,

> "The conditions that preserve dark suffering are the result of hundreds of years and multiple continents' commitment to creating and maintaining destructive, insidious, racist ideals that uphold white supremacy and anti-Blackness. The field of education is anchored in white rage, especially public education" (p.22)

To this end, we contend that not interrupting this legacy of oppression, especially when you have the tools, resources, and access, is a perpetuation of white supremacy.

Edmund: What are your overall thoughts on the field of hip-hop and education? What inspires you about the field right now?

Dr. Runell Hall: So, I think what's interesting to me is that we have so many scholars now who have been able to put their voices into the mix. I would say with AERA and other organizations, that's how things become codified. They become institutionalized and a part of the conversation when you have these different elements represented in those spaces. So that's very heartening to me. I feel that means those of us who might have felt like we were on the margins when we were starting have began to feel like, maybe it's okay, that we're moving a little bit more to the center. It's a little more centered. Like anything else, though, particularly when it has its origins in Black and Brown communities, there is always the risk of things getting, you know, commodified or co-opted in ways that are not about liberation that are not going to be ultimately serving the students and communities that we would hope they would. Cause you could use hip-hop and still teach in oppressive pedagogical ways, and you could still be reinforcing oppressive dynamics and just doing it in a way that has students more interested, which actually to me is reprehensible because that's actually manipulative, right? That's the sort of bringing students in on something that they feel is their culture and then sort of making it about actually reinforcing dominant culture. I think we've come really far. I think we still have to make sure the guardrails and the critical lens are always present. If it starts to feel like they're not, then we, we need, there needs to be the right checks and balances. So that it's not just, well, because we rhymed a lesson. Therefore it is now hip-hop pedagogy.

Dr. Marcella Runell Hall cautions that while hip-hop education is rooted in liberatory, social-justice oriented conceptualizations of education, if not done with fidelity, hip-hop education has the potential to reproduce harm. This harm is evident in the educator that waters down aspects of hip-hop culture or positions hip-hop as a pedagogical "hook" that seeks to entice students into engaging with the traditional whitewashed curriculum (Evans, Turner & Allen, 2020). To this point Evans, Turner and Allen (2020), contend,

> "Too often, schools "repackage" the cultures of students and use it to perpetuate routines and academic standards set by the school—reminiscent of how the corporate hip-hop industry has stolen the culture of hip-hop youth to repackage and sell it in a manner that solely feeds the interests of corporate hip-hop (Emdin & Adjapong, 2018, p. 1). We see this repackaging of students' culture as an incarnation of interest convergence wherein issues of race, and equity is only addressed if and when they converge with the interests and expectations of white ideologies (Bell, 1980; Milner, 2008). As such, students' cultures can only exist within the classroom to the extent with which the educator understands and is comfortable" (p. 58).

To separate hip-hop from its roots in social justice and liberatory education is a misappropriation of hip-hop education and is an act of curricular violence. In recognizing hip-hop as Black culture (Blair, 2004), we acknowledge that the weaponization of hip-hop education is most often inflicted upon Black students as a form of anti-Black violence. Anti-Black violence in schools is expressed in educational research (i.e., Boutte & Bryan, 2019; Johnson, Bryan & Boutte, 2018) and can take many forms. Johnson et al. (2018) outline five types of anti-Black violence in schools: physical, symbolic, linguistic, curricular/pedagogical, and systemic school violence. A definition and example of each type of violence are outlined in the Table 5.1. Utilizing the definition of curricular and pedagogical violence given by Johnson et al. (2018), separating hip-hop education from its roots in liberatory education and social justice is, indeed, violence. Not only does this separation re-center white notions of existing and being in the world, but it also creates the potential to "eliminate critical conversations about race, gender, religion, language, sexuality, etc." and allows the educator to potentially "unintentionally and/or intentionally minimize how teacher positionality shapes curricular decisions and pedagogical practices" (Johnson et al., 2018). Because of this danger, we contend that all hip-hop educational practices must be rooted in critical understandings of social justice and liberatory education to avoid the perpetuation of curricular violence in schools.

Table 5.1. Types of Anti-Black Violence in Urban Schools

Types of Violence	Definition	Examples
Physical	The physical abuse and assault that stem from racial discrimination and prejudicial ideologies and beliefs	• Hitting, pushing, beating, etc. • Lynching • Police brutality • Sexual abuse and sexual assault
Symbolic	A metaphorical representation of violence that stems from, "racial abuse, pain, and suffering against the spirit and humanity of Black people" (Author, under review)	• Racial epithets and slurs • Rejecting the experiences and lived realities of Black youth • Silencing the voices of Black youth • (mis)reading Black youths' culture, race, gender, and language
Linguistic	This form of violence marginalizes and polices the language of Black youth which is referred to as (e.g., Black language, African American language, or African American Vernacular English) through privileging and promoting white mainstream English	• Socializing Black youth to view Black language as "not good", "broken English", and "incorrect" • Devaluing the connection between language, race, and identity
Curricular and Pedagogical	This form of violence infiltrates schools' curriculum through teaching texts, materials, and standards that center Eurocratic notions of existing and being in the world (Cridland-Hughes and King, 2015). In conjunction, the conventional curriculum provides a false narrative about Black people through promoting deficit-based ideologies which	• Enacting culturally irrelevant and unresponsive curriculum • Selecting texts where Black youth do not see characters who look like them reflected in dynamic and positive ways • Feeding Black youth inaccurate, distorted, diluted, incomplete, and sanitized versions of history, math, and science

Types of Violence	Definition	Examples
	inform teachers' pedagogical and instructional practices in classrooms. In general, this is a form of epistemic violence which attacks Black ways of knowing.	• Omitting critical conversations from the curriculum that explore the intersections of race, gender, religion, language, sexuality, etc. • Unintentionally and/or intentionally minimizing how teacher positionality shapes curricular decisions and pedagogical practices
Systemic school	This form of violence is deeply ingrained within schools' structures, processes, discourses, customs, policies, and laws which oftentimes reflect racist and hegemonic ideologies	• Underfunded and overcrowded schools • Inexperienced teachers and/or teachers who are not certified in the subject area(s) they teach • Overrepresentation of Black youth in special education courses • Tracking • Disproportionality of Black youth in gifted and talented courses • Zero tolerance school discipline policies • Lack of educational and support services that promote a positive healthy development—physically, mentally, and emotional

Edmund: In your opinion, what challenges persist in the field of hip-hop and education? Or are there challenges that you've experienced that might persist currently in the field?

Dr. Russell Hall: I think there's always this tension around appropriation versus appreciation, right? This idea that if we give too many, too many tools, if we push this too much that then we have people appropriating in ways that would actually be alienating and offensive to young people who identify as part of hip-hop. And that's a fine line. I mean, I see it with my own kids, like where they feel validated and like an authentic connection with the teacher who may or may not know anything about what they're interested in. Versus the teachers who pretend as if they know. And then it becomes like they've violated a sacred space.

> I'm cautious of always feeling like we put this out into the world, and we ask people to embrace this as a methodology, as a pedagogy, and to respect that this is a culture that has many levels and types and many layers. So it's been youth culture, but we've all grown up in it too. So what does that mean when you're not 15 anymore? So I guess for me, it's that, how do we maintain a sacredness around this while still promoting that this is important for educators to know and learn for the wellbeing, and the care, and the engagement of our young people.

As Dr. Runell Hall explains, we must consider how we navigate the line between misappropriation and appreciation in hip-hop education. While we do not claim to hold all of the answers as to how to achieve this, we contend that educational research on hip-hop education may hold some answers for us. For example, educational research has demonstrated that a key piece in being effective hip-hop pedagogues is being willing to critically reflect on yourself, your positionality, and the pedagogy you employ (Irby & Hall, 2011; Kelly & Sawyer, 2019). At times, this may be uncomfortable because it can reveal spaces of disconnect between your intention in your pedagogy and how students perceive it (Irby & Hall, 2011; Kelly & Sawyer, 2019). As explained by Buffington and Day (2018), engaging in hip-hop education requires educators to "question what knowledge looks like and where and how it circulates" and "de-center themselves and their knowledge" (Buffington & Day, 2018, p. 9). It can be a potentially difficult task to decenter oneself in the classroom because that requires a relinquishing of control that is not commonly advocated for in traditional teacher education programs or schooling spaces.

Kelly: We've been grappling with that a lot. What I'm interested in is, from your perspective and identifying as white, how do you go about discussing that, particularly with other white educators who may be interested in doing this work? How do you approach that conversation?

Dr. Runell Hall: I think there has to be some kind of built-in opportunity for professional development, learning, and unlearning around race and racism. And then an intersectional approach to that, of course. So not leaving it that it's just about race and racism, because there are other aspects. In my very first few minutes of introducing myself to you, I was trying to kind of signal like it is intersectional. It does matter, right? These identities do matter to us. I think that for people who have a lot of privileged identities—particularly around race, often, that's considered to be normal or invisible or not named—there's that piece around getting the work, whatever you need, whatever that looks like in terms of curriculum, training, reading, accountability, to be able to talk about race. I think you should not even be trying to teach hip-hop if you haven't done that work on yourself. So that's a prerequisite I would say is, you know, there's a lot of people out there doing really good work around learning and unlearning race and racism. It's lifelong work. Like we're socialized in it. This is the social environment that we are all swimming in. I think there needs to be that level of commitment around doing the work on yourself.

Dr. Runell Hall articulates the necessity of individuals, particularly those with privileged identities, doing deep and critical self-work before engaging in hip-hop education. Especially given that hip-hop culture was created to be a tool to promote social justice and advocate for the needs of historically marginalized communities, you must "do the courageous and important work of looking at yourself and what you know before you grab onto the brilliant curriculum frameworks in the Black tradition" (Dillard, 2022, p. 181). Therefore we contend that it is imperative that individuals with privileged identities understand not only the history of hip-hop but an understanding of their own identities and how they intersect with the hip-hop populations they engage with. This understanding is important because

> "as the person responsible for your student's well-being and wholeness in mind, body, and spirit, you too must be whole…not perfect, but having spent considerable time in reflection, careful study, and examination of your spirit, your knowledge of the children you teach, and the values embedded in the long traditions of their people" (Dillard, 2022, p. 180).

In order for educators to engage in authentic and effective hip-hop and education research and/or praxis, there must be an interrogation of positionality (including racial identity), and how this positionality relates to and interacts with institutions, systems, and the hip-hop populations the individual is engaged with. It must be remembered, however, that "it is impossible not to have some racial knowledge and teach about it within a racial state such as the United States…yet the concern is what racial knowledge is accepted as fact" (King, 2022, p. ix). To this end, it must be understood that there is no such thing as neutrality in this work. Further, we have all been matriculated through systems that privilege whiteness, and therefore we must all engage in this important and critical work of understanding who we are in relation to hip-hop culture and the hip-hop populations we engage with.

Because of the extent that whiteness has been normalized in our society, this work of "looking at yourself and what you know," as Dillard (2022) states, must be a layered process. Sealey-Ruiz (2021) provides insight into what this layered process might look like through the articulation of six components to racial literacy development: critical love, critical humility, critical reflection, historical literacy, archaeology of self, and interruption, as identified in Figure 5.1 below. Racial literacy "promotes deep self-examination and requires actions that can lead to sustainable social justice and educational equity for all students" (Sealey-Ruiz, 2021, p. 5). The goal of this self-examination is to foster deeper, more constructive conversations around race, racism, and racial equity in schools (Sealey-Ruiz, 2021).

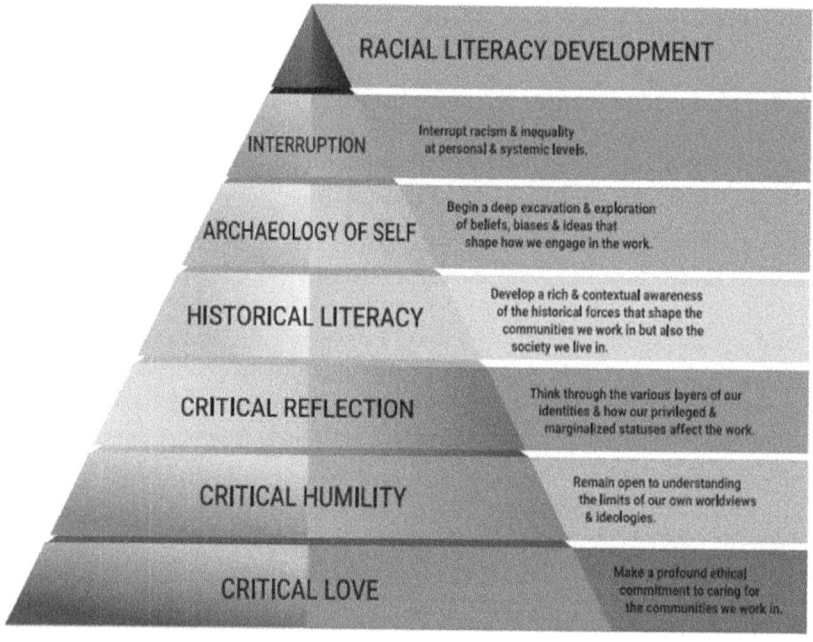

Figure 5.1: Racial Literacy Development Model

Edmund: We're curious if you can share with us how you focus on hip-hop culture and history and how you leverage that in your work to create opportunities for social change. And if you want, you can speak to the intersections of hip-hop and social justice.

Dr. Runell Hall: If we were to look at hip-hop in the continuum from, even if we just went to recent times, like the Black arts movement and thinking about the role of arts in activism and arts and social justice, I think that's the continuum that most speaks to me. How I engaged with hip-hop when I was 12 is different than when I was 22. And the Lord knows it's different now that I'm 47. So it's not the case that

I know everything in the same way that I did. I think there are different ways to engage. For me, I would say that that's been the important part to not hold myself to an unrealistic standard and think that I'm still gonna engage with the culture in the same ways at every stage of my life. I think that's true for lots of people. The second thing I would say is that looking at the continuum in terms of arts and activism, that's a part of me that I don't think will ever go away. I'm always, always fascinated by the role that music plays in movements and the way that culture, youth culture in particular, shapes activism.

Edmund: I'm curious about your positionality as a woman who engages in hip-hop scholarship. In understanding the reality of patriarchy, what advice do you have for scholars?

Dr. Runell Hall: So one of the things that I would first lift up that has been so helpful to me being in a gender-diverse women's college space is even problematizing and interrogating concepts around gender. Just thinking more about how different people are marginalized and oppressed around gender that aren't necessarily on the binary. I would add to the conversation that when I first was coming up in hip-hop, there was a lot that felt really homophobic and transphobic and complicated around gender and hip-hop. I think that some of that is still there because much of that is still in society, and we reflect that. In terms of my own identity and being a woman in the space, I would say that I always had mentors. I always had relationships with other women who were participating in the culture, either as writers or journalists or artists, or they were in the business end, or the creative arts end, or the fashion end, or, I mean, there were a million and one different ways that I saw women participating in hip-hop. That just reinforced for me what my little middle school self had learned from Salt-N-Pepa and others, like MC Lyte. I believe that that's how it should be, and that's how it was, you know what I mean? But those were mostly all women of color. I would say that that's a really important part of the narrative. The centering of women of color in hip-hop and the idea that we can complicate this binary and think about gender oppression and other connections and intersectionality around sexual orientation and gender feels really important in all of that. So for me, I felt like I had a lot of role models and a lot of support. I still feel like that now. But I think there's a lot of people that have written about their own complicated relationship with hip-hop and to misogyny and patriarchy, but also needing to push back against it and like both things can be true.

Dr. Runell Hall acknowledges the challenges that persist in hip-hop culture in relation to misogyny and patriarchy. She highlights that in discussions about how oppression fueled by misogyny and patriarchy manifests in hip-hop, we also must recognize how folks outside of the gender binary experience oppression. This is an important emphasis because individuals who identify beyond the binary experience violence and harassment in every aspect of life at higher rates (James et al., 2016) and have limited access to systems of support (Hester et al., 2012). While scholars discuss and interrogate the experiences of women and Black feminism in relationship to hip-hop (Durham, Cooper & Morris, 2013; Love, 2012), scholarly interrogations of individuals who identify outside the gender binary are limited. While there are challenges specific to women in hip-hop that are largely documented (Perry, 2003), there are also challenges related to homophobia and transphobia within hip-hop culture. We acknowledge that hip-hop provides a space to interrogate anti-Blackness, but many hip-hop spaces have been constructed on hetero-patriarchal, misogynistic, homophobic, and transphobic ideals that ultimately oppress Black women, trans, and queer people, and non-gender conforming folx (Durham et al., 2013; Love, 2016). The hip-hop community, including scholars and educators, must reorient our various lenses to consider and explore the realities of individuals who identify outside the gender binary. We must challenge hip-hop as a culture to counter instances of violence against individuals who identify outside the gender binary with the goal of being inclusive of groups that experience high rates of violence in society writ large.

Edmund:	If you could radically dream about the future of hip-hop and education, what would you envision?
Dr. Runell Hall:	I would envision for young people coming up that they have teachers, educators and administrators, and adults who have done the work to be able to really bring the beauty and the magic and the complexity and the uniqueness of hip-hop into educational spaces with care. It's no longer enough to say, "teachers need to engage in this work." Teachers need to do the work and have the right tools and training, and support to do this in ways that maintain sacredness and allow students to feel safe, share parts of themselves and be able to see themselves in the work. Then I would say for our young people that we're always trying to do our best to be better than whoever came before us and that we, we owe that to them.

Dr. Runell Hall's freedom dream is that more teachers and school administrators recognize the power and potential of utilizing hip-hop in a critical way within educational contexts. Since its conception, Hip-Hop culture continues to be used as a vehicle to promote social justice and advocate for the needs of historically marginalized communities. Many scholars and educators have leveraged the use of hip-hop culture and sensibilities within educational spaces to support the call for cultural responsiveness within schools and as an opportunity to support the development of youths' critical consciousness (Muhammad, 2013; Young, Young, Cason et al., 2018). Further, Dr. Runell Hall dreams that educators position themselves to engage in the pre-work necessary to effectively and appropriately engage their students in hip-hop and education. Recognizing that not all educators will have a natural affinity towards hip-hop culture, a culture that was created and innovated by Black communities, it's imperative that educators interrogate their positionality to understand and eliminate the possible bias that they may have of hip-hop, and as a result, of Black people. This work is possible, but it takes educators to first recognize the power of hip-hop culture and, second, a willingness to engage in the self-work necessary to be empowered to create actual change.

To learn more about Dr. Marcella Runell Hall's research and scholarship, check out the following:

- Hall, M. R. (2011). Education in a hip-hop nation: Our identity, politics & pedagogy. Amherst: The University of Massachusetts.
- Hall, M. R. (2009). Hip-Hop education resources. *Equity & Excellence in Education, 42*(1), 86–94.
- Runell, M., & Diaz, M. (2007). *The hip hop education guidebook: Volume 1.* The Hip Hop Association, Inc.

References

Adjapong, E. (2017). Bridging theory and practice in the urban science classroom: A framework for hip-hop pedagogy. Critical Education, 8(15), 5–23. http://ojs.library.ubc.ca/index.php/criticaled/article/view/186248

Blair, M. E. (2004). Commercialization of the rap music youth subculture. That's the Joint, 497–499.

Boutte, G., & Bryan, N. (2021). When will Black children be well? Interrupting anti-Black violence in early childhood classrooms and schools. Contemporary Issues in Early Childhood, 22(3), 232–243.

Bridget, K., & Winkle-Wagner, R. (2017). Finding a voice in predominantly white institutions: A longitudinal study of Black women faculty members' journeys toward tenure. Teachers College Record, 119(6), 1–36.

Buffington, M. L., & Day, J. (2018). Hip-Hop pedagogy as culturally sustaining pedagogy. Arts, 7(97), 1–11. https://doi.org/10.3390/arts7040097.

Chang, J. (2007). *Can't stop won't stop: A history of the Hip Hop generation.* St. Martin's Press.

Croom, N. N. (2017). Promotion beyond tenure: Unpacking racism and sexism in the experiences of Black womyn professors. *Review of Higher Education, 40*(4), 557–583.

Dillard, C. B. (2022). *The spirit of our work: Black women teachers (re)member.* Beacon Press.

Durham, A., Cooper, B. C., & Morris, S. M. (2013). The stage hip-hop feminism built: A new directions essay. *Signs: Journal of Women in Culture and Society, 38*(3), 721–737.

Evans, L., Turner, C., & Allen, K. R. (2020). "Good Teachers" with "Good Intentions": Misappropriations of culturally responsive pedagogy. *Journal of Urban Learning, Teaching & Research, 15*(1), 51–73.

Garrison-Wade, D. F., Diggs, G. A., Estrada, D., & Galindo, R. (2012). Lift every voice and sing: Faculty of color face the challenges of the tenure track. *Urban Review: Issues and Ideas in Public Education, 44*(1), 90–112.

Gibson, A., Hughes-Hassell, S., & Threats, M. (2017). Critical race theory in the LIS curriculum. In J. Percell, L. C. Sarin, P. T. Jaeger, & J. C. Bertot (Eds.), *Re-envisioning the MLS: Perspectives on the future of library and information science education* (pp. 49–70). Emerald.

Gibson, A. N. (2019). Civility and structural precarity for faculty of color in LIS. *Journal of Education for Library and Information Science, 60*(3), 215–222.

Haynes, C., Taylor, L., Mobley, S. D., & Haywood, J. (2020). Existing and resisting: The pedagogical realities of Black, critical men and women faculty. *Journal of Higher Education, 91*(5), 698–721.

Hester, M., Williamson, E., Regan, L., Coulter, M., Chantler, K., Gangoli, G.,... & Green, L. (2012). *Exploring the service and support needs of male, lesbian, gay, bi-sexual and transgendered and Black and other minority ethnic victims of domestic and sexual violence.* Bristol: University of Bristol.

James, S., Herman, J., Rankin, S., Keisling, M., Mottet, L., & Anafi, M. A. (2016). *The report of the 2015 US transgender survey.*

Johnson, L. L., Bryan, N., & Boutte, G. (2019). Show us the love: Revolutionary teaching in (un) critical times. *The Urban Review, 51,* 46–64.

King, L. J. (2022). Introduction: Social studies, all things race, and racism. In L. J. King (Ed.), *Racial literacies and social studies: Curriculum, instruction and learning.* Teachers College Press.

Laura, L. J. (2019). Faculty of Color unmask color-blind ideology in the community college faculty search process. *Community College Journal of Research and Practice, 43*(10–11), 702–717.

Levin, J. S., Jackson-Boothby, A., Haberler, Z., & Walker, L. (2015). "Dangerous work": Improving conditions for faculty of color in the community college. *Community College Journal of Research and Practice, 39*(9), 852–864.

Love, B. (2012). *Hip-Hop's lil' sistas speak: Negotiating hip-hop identities and politics in the New South.* New York, NY: Peter Lang.

Love, B. (2016). Complex personhood of hip hop & the sensibilities of the culture that fosters knowledge of self & self-determination. *Equity & Excellence in Education, 49*(4), 414–427.

Love, B. (2019). *We want to do more than survive: Abolitionist teaching and the pursuit of educational freedom.* Beacon Press.

Perry, I. (2003). Who(se) am I? The identity and image of women in hip hop. In G. Dines & J. M. Humez (Eds.), *Gender, race, and class in media: A text reader* (2nd ed., pp. 136-148). Thousand Oaks, CA: Sage.

Petchauer, E. (2009). Framing and reviewing hip hop educational research. *Review of Educational Research, 79*(2), 946–978. https://doi.org/10.3102/0034654308330967.

Rose, T. (1994). *Black noise: Rap music and Black culture in contemporary America*. Wesleyan University Press.

Runell, M., & Diaz, M. (2007). *The hip hop education guidebook: Volume 1*. The Hip Hop Association, Inc.

Sealey-Ruiz, Y. (2020). The racial literacy development model. Arch of self. https://www.yolandasealeyruiz.com/archaeology-of-self

Tanner, S. J. (2019). Whiteness is a white problem: Whiteness in English education. *English Education, 51*(2), 182–199.

· 6 ·

ON YOUTH-CENTERED HIP-HOP PEDAGOGIES AND PRAXIS: KEEPING IT REAL WITH LAUREN KELLY

Dr. Lauren Leigh Kelly is an Assistant Professor of Urban Education at Rutgers University's Graduate School of Education. Dr. Kelly received her Ph.D. in English Education from Teachers College, Columbia University. Her work focuses on adolescent critical literacy development, Black feminist theory, hip-hop pedagogy, critical consciousness, and the development of critical, culturally sustaining pedagogies. She is also the director of the annual youth-led Hip-Hop Youth Research and Activism conference.

Edmund:	Thanks for taking the time to meet with us, Lauren. Let's jump in. To start off, can you explain what shapes your identity as a scholar?
Dr. Lauren Kelly:	I would say my identity as a scholar really emerges from my identity as an educator, first and foremost. So my work as a scholar is ultimately trying to impact the classroom. I want to make sure my research is not just something that's cited in papers. It needs to get through to teachers and into the lives of students. And so that is really my goal as a scholar. My work is speaking to audiences of teachers and young people. I want a 15-year-old to be able to read my work and understand it and not be like, "I don't know what this is." I think it's limiting if our work doesn't speak to the audiences we care about, right? If BIPOC youth in K-12 education and even undergraduates can't connect to my work, then that's not really

helpful; then I'm not in conversation with them. I think we fall into that trap of speaking *about* rather than *with* young folk and BIPOC communities. I also think that if teachers can't access the work—if they feel like, "Okay, I need to be taking a college class to be reading this," or this is just about, you know, sort of citations, intellectualism, and theories and not actually about planning lessons and what I do on Tuesday in the classroom, then we miss that audience too. I think if our scholarship is about classrooms and engaging with classroom spaces, then we need to speak and write and care about classrooms in a way that impacts that audience.

Edmund: As an individual, how do you align yourself with hip-hop culture in your work?

Dr. Lauren Kelly: I think that shifts all the time. As someone who is not a young person anymore, I don't think I can claim a sort of youth hip-hop identity. I have one inside myself from the nineties and early two thousands. But at the end of the day, I'm aware that there are ways in which I don't share the same identities as young people, even the same hip-hop identities as young people, and I think that's important to acknowledge. So it has shifted over time. When I first started doing work in the hip-hop education space, specifically in the classroom, it was because I did share a lot of those identities with my students. We listened to a lot of the same music, or their older siblings listened to the same stuff I listened to. So it really was sort of an organic approach to connecting with young people, just sharing our identities in this collective space. Building community through hip-hop culture, which includes not just music, but language. Talking about, you know, artists within the hip-hop community and history, or even just thinking about the ethos of hip-hop. But I think over time, as I have, I guess, grown into this scholar identity and researcher identity, it's much more about taking that sort of knowledge-of-self approach and the hip-hop ethos approach to working with young people and to doing research. You know, if I talk about, let's say someone like Method Man, that just doesn't have the same relevance for young people now. And so I would say my hip-hop identities have shifted, and at this point, are more about really connecting to, you know, hip-hop as a form of culture and community with young people, as opposed to really specific expertise around artists or lyrics.

Dr. Lauren Leigh Kelly wants her research to be accessible to teachers and students. A key part of achieving this goal is using language that is accessible to teachers and students so the research can be applied in the classroom. Another key piece of this is ensuring that she is rooted in knowledge of self. While Dr. Lauren Leigh Kelly initially began exploring the intersections of hip-hop and education because she shared similar hip-hop identities as the young people she worked with, she recognizes that as time goes on, her hip-hop identity continues to evolve. A key part of ensuring that her work focused on hip-hop education is accessible and relevant to teachers and students is acknowledging that her hip-hop identity has evolved over time and may not parallel that of her students.

Edmund: In your opinion, what might be some qualifications to engage in hip-hop and education work for teachers, scholars, researchers, etc.?

Dr. Lauren Kelly: I think it depends on the person. At the end of the day, I don't think you need to be a certain person to teach hip-hop, but I do think you have to commit to young people and to equity and social justice. If you're brand new to this and you're like, "I barely listen to hip-hop. I've heard of Cardi B", then cool! I'm so glad you're excited about this. I don't want teachers to say, "well, I don't come from this. I don't identify as a hip-hop head, so I can't teach this." But I think you have to be really mindful about how you go about this work. You have to invite people in—people who have, you know, extensive background or knowledge, training, experience, whatever it is, in this work, and you have to make sure they're being adequately compensated.

And you also have to invite young people in. And everyone should do that regardless of how hip-hop identified they are. I think as long as you're an adult, you're already a little bit distant from youth culture, right? And so you always need to have young people inform your curriculum. But I think the more distanced you are from hip-hop culture, having that language and that knowledge, the more people you need to invite into your curriculum writing and your lesson design, including young people. And the goal is not for you to be an expert, like, "Now let me get a degree in hip-hop so I can teach it". You just have to be an expert at gathering the right people and listening to your students. And listening to the people that you're gathering. Then bringing your pedagogical expertise, your math or science or health, whatever your specialty is. But leave that hip-hop expertise to the people that you're inviting in.

For Dr. Lauren Leigh Kelly, foundational to hip-hop education is an equity-oriented, youth-centered approach to education. A focus on youth is important when engaging in hip-hop education because, at its core, youth continue to be at the forefront of innovation in hip-hop and must be at the center of all we do in educational spaces. As Dr. Lauren Leigh Kelly notes, this means that we must be willing to bring youth into the conversation around hip-hop education and center them in the curriculum design and pedagogical implementation of hip-hop education. Simultaneously, we must recognize that hip-hop education rejects traditional teaching strategies and school curricula that are rooted in western views and Eurocentric frameworks that position whiteness as the center of legitimate knowledge. An important part of this pursuit of equity is a grounding in knowledge of self. This is particularly imperative when bringing hip-hop into educational spaces because hip-hop's element *knowledge of self* encourages participants of hip-hop culture to be aware and critical of who they are, be authentic to themselves and their identities, and be confident in themselves to make positive social-political change for their communities (Adjapong, 2017). In order for educators to engage in authentic and effective hip-hop educational research and/or praxis, there must be an examination of positionality and how this positionality relates to and interacts with institutions, systems, and the hip-hop populations the individual is engaged with. Dr. Lauren Leigh Kelly recognizes that an embodiment of knowledge of self includes being cognizant that teachers and researchers—herself included—cannot do this work without listening to students. But is this critical self-work something that all educators are ready to do?

Edmund: I definitely think that if an educator wants to engage in this work, they have to have the critical aptitude to understand the realities around Blackness and the culture to effectively engage. But also, the other side of me is just like, when do we get to the point where we can actually get teachers to actively engage in this work where it's not like pulling teeth? I've engaged in workshops, I've talked at schools, and I've worked with teachers who want to engage in hip-hop and education. They want to do the work. But then they hear someone talk about, "Okay, this is how we situate ourselves in the work." And teachers are like, "Oh, that's a lot of work. I haven't thought about that." I guess that's the part I always get to, and I'm like, "Damn!" This obviously can be so impactful for so many young people, but in my experience, at least as an educator and teacher educator, is that a lot of folks don't want to pick it up because of the self-reflection and personal interrogation work that it entails. And that's part of the work, too, right?

Dr. Lauren Kelly: All of that is true. I will say, I think the focus that I have on inviting young people into the conversation, for me, means you actually don't have to do that much. You just have to have faith in your students. Because it's not going to work if you don't trust them. And you have to create the space, which means maybe 20 minutes

	on a Tuesday. Maybe having students stay after one day a month or one day a week. But I don't think you actually need to, like, read all of the books and listen to the whole discography of Jay-Z. As a teacher, I actually think you just have to find the time in the curriculum or in the schedule for the week, and trust students and invite them. I don't personally think it's that much work. I think it just feels intimidating.
Edmund:	No, I get that. But is a teacher who doesn't have a critical lens going to listen to students who are critical? The teacher may not understand or even be open to listening to students' perspectives. I've worked with other scholars who believe that it's not the students' responsibility to teach their teacher, who's licensed and received "training". There's always going to be that duality, right?
	I think, yeah, this work can happen within the community and it can happen in collaboration. But back to the idea of criticality. If I'm a Black student, I have a white teacher who's wants to use hip-hop in their instruction, and asks me to, "come share about your Blackness so I can gain some insight so we can create something collaboratively to facilitate together." Still feels like a lot of labor for the student. But while I agree that students shouldn't take on the brunt of the work, I do think it's necessary for students to be involved because if we're teaching through hip-hop we still need to understand how students relate and connect to hip-hop.
Kelly:	Yeah, but to your point, Lauren, —I think it's easy for those of us that *do* trust our students—I think the issue is that our current educational system and the way we operate in schools makes it so teachers are conditioned to not trust their students.
Edmund:	Facts.
Kelly:	I think the current educational system encourages teachers to say, "I have this control, and I'm not giving it up because if I do give up this control, it will be chaos." And so I think for teachers who have accepted that "Yeah, I do trust my students, and they have these really knowledgeable and generative thoughts," then yeah, I think it could be easier. But I think that the trouble that you're talking about, Edmund, is like a lot of teachers truly buy into the way the current system operates, so what do we do?
Dr. Lauren Kelly:	Yeah, that's true.

The core of successfully implementing hip-hop education, according to Dr. Kelly, is having trust in students. What does it mean, then, to be ready to engage in hip-hop education if current schooling norms place teachers in positions where they are conditioned not to trust students? America's schools are known to criminalize students, particularly Black, Brown and systemically marginalized groups, which often stems from misunderstanding of students' realities and lack of trust in students (Thompson, 2011). However, the question remains: what are the implications of this process when the field is full of predominantly white teachers whose practices are rooted in white supremacy and anti-Blackness? Maxine Greene (1988) contends that a part of education is engaging in a continual process of "making deeply personal choices about who you are and who you will become as a teacher" (p. 12). Therefore, the process of becoming "ready" to engage in hip-hop education praxis must entail a deep excavation of the self and the self in relation to the educational structures teachers and students exist within. This continual process of becoming ready requires educators to intentionally engage in a process of identifying and unlearning oppressive practices and intentionally choosing to center equity and justice in their practice.

Edmund: We know that in your work, you advocate for the centering of pedagogy and curriculum on youth self-actualization versus the tangible artifacts of hip-hop culture. We wanted you to talk more about this point, and what do you think educators and researchers can do to encourage the self-actualization of young people in classroom settings or educational settings at large?

Dr. Lauren Kelly: I'm glad you asked this. I think this is that difference between the sort of more superficial approaches to utilizing hip-hop in schools. For example, "we read a Jay-Z song together" or "we watched a Cardi B video." And I think young people can be very trusting of educators, so if they had a fun classroom experience, they're not really likely to send you an email and say: "You did not engage with our identities and our self-reflection." I think it is even hard for an educator to gauge if they're doing this work. I think it's three things.

One is creating a space in a classroom that is trusting. We have to create trusting classroom spaces, really in any class, but especially I would say, with hip-hop and education. Because if you're really doing critical work in the hip-hop and education space, it gets messy, right? We're dealing with issues of race, class, gender and power, and sexuality. All of these things come up inevitably if you're doing this right and well. And so there has to be a classroom space that is trusting, that allows for students to share their ideas, their questions, and their uncertainties. Because if students are closed up, if they feel like they have to present a certain persona, or if they're just there to show off like how cool they are, and their hip-hop knowledge, you won't really get anywhere, especially towards self-actualization. So creating a community space where students feel like they trust their teacher, they trust each other, and they can build towards trusting themselves to share.

Second, there have to be particular assignments. These don't necessarily have to be like essays, right? Assignments can take the place of or contain multiple forms. As Kelly has written about, as you've written about, Edmund, it could be playlists. It could be mixtapes. They could be videos, or really creative assignments. But assignments that really force students to go beyond that superficial thing. So moving beyond, like, you know, "write an essay about Cardi B" or "create a project that shares all of your favorite songs." But there has to be a prompt in there that forces them to really engage with and reflect on their own values and identities. Rather than, "write an essay about Doja Cat" or "give a presentation on her rise to fame," maybe the topic is more about, you know, a presentation on how she engages with notions of Black femininity. Because then what that forces you to do as a student is you have to go beyond—you can engage with her lyrics, and pull out specific quotes, pull out things from her life—but you also have to engage with theories of Black femininity. It's going to be hard to write that paper and not have some reference to someone like bell hooks. But then you also have to think about your own identities, who you are and how you engage with that. So I think having assignments that are really intentional in having students move beyond the superficial, move beyond their expertise, move beyond what they know, and start to engage with identities and theories.

Third is in discussions. That's what I've written a lot about with the class that I taught, is that it was very discussion based. It was not a lot of lecturing. It wasn't a lot of students lecturing or me lecturing, but it was a lot of us sitting in a circle, sometimes in rows, and just having conversations on what we were hearing and what that meant, and sitting in the discomfort of people having different takeaways. So, you know, Edmund may have loved Kendrick's album, and Kelly might say, "I don't know, it's a little too preachy for me, I don't think that's what music should do." And then now we're having this 40-minute discussion around, not even Kendrick, but what should music be doing? Is it okay for music to feel like a book sometimes? And, of course, there's no right answer, right? All of it is subjective. But it's really about coming closer to yourself and understanding who you are and what you care about in that conversation. And I don't think that happens without the community space. This goes back to sort of the first point about the community. If that's just a homework assignment, you'll get somewhere, right? And maybe the assignment is, you know, "what should music do?" But you only really come to your own understandings about yourself in that dialogue, and by someone challenging your ideas. Someone presenting new ideas, and you having to theorize out loud with the community that you trust about what it is that you're thinking and feeling and why. And so I think those are the three pieces that really lead to self-actualization happening in the classroom, specifically through hip-hop education.

Dr. Lauren Leigh Kelly's finding that classroom spaces must be built on trust before engaging in hip-hop education echoes the findings by Love (2016) in the article titled *Complex Personhood of Hip Hop & the Sensibilities of the Culture that Fosters Knowledge of Self & Self-Determination*. Through her examination of hip-hop educational spaces, Love (2016) found that essential to critical engagement in hip-hop education were spaces where, "youth were not under surveillance and criminalized for being Black, they were given the space to create. Moreover, the space was filled with adults or youth leaders who were selected by the community…who recognized that young people had the sensibilities, performance acumen, and power to "represent, recognize, come correct, and build, maintain, respect" (Morgan, 2009, pp. 15–16), which are the foundational origins of hip-hop" (p. 423).

Another core piece of self-actualization through hip-hop education is engaging students in critical examinations of hip-hop that reject the hyper-commercialization of hip-hop education. Just as hip-hop culture has become commercialized, as hip-hop education has gained popularity, it has fallen into the throws of commercialization. In recognizing this, Love (2016) writes,

> Prepackaged hip-hop education products remove and dismiss the culture, history, elements, sensibilities, and ideas that students can critically examine hip-hop culture's violent, homophobic, and sexist messages to form new knowledge and imagine new possibilities for justice in exchange for a reduced singular definition of hip-hop. Through this lens, hip-hop is not seen as a culture with a rich history that should be shared with all students, regardless of race, ethnicity, and class through hip-hop education, but instead as a teaching framework for students of color labeled as academically and culturally deficit. Thus, much of the hip-hop educational products are constructed through the colonizing enterprise of educational research.

To combat this superficial implementation of hip-hop education, Dr. Kelly discusses potential pedagogical alternatives that encourage students to engage in critical discussions, reflections, and thought around sociocultural phenomena. A key piece of this is engaging students in dialogue. Through the dialogic process, self-actualization can be activated because dialogic action supports the process of knowing as means towards liberation (Freire, 2012).

Edmund: Lauren, if you can radically dream about the future of hip-hop in education, what would you envision?

Dr. Lauren Kelly: I'm a very impatient person. So anything that I radically dream about, I try to start right away. So I'm working on my radical vision of hip-hop education's future, and that is similar to what we were just discussing. It's young people really leading it. Not in ways that are exploitative or extractive of them. The project that I'm starting in September through the NAEd/Spencer Postdoctoral Fellowship is actually bringing young people together. They're going to be provided with food and travel and stipends and all of the things so it's not exploitative or extractive. But it's bringing people together, sort of like a think tank, to think about what are youth-informed approaches to teaching. What have they learned from their experiences as students? These are high school and college students, sort of a range of experiences. What have they learned? What works for them? What doesn't work? And from this youth-informed lens, how can teachers learn from them about how to do this work better. How to create classrooms that are humanizing, that respond to young people, and that respond to young people's futures. So they come together to share their ideas, brainstorm, get some training in sort of critical and arts-infused approaches to teaching. Then they're developing a professional development for teachers, where the teachers show up and learn from young people. That is, that is my radical vision, is that teachers are actually learning from young people. I think we can do it. But it does require, like, as you were saying, Kelly, trust, and faith in young people.

Dr. Lauren Leigh Kelly's radical dream for the field of hip-hop education is for the further development of critical, youth-centered approaches to hip-hop praxis and pedagogy. Kelly is taking up her radical dream with the support of a National Academy of Education and Spencer Foundation fellowship where she is interrogating the experiences of youth of color as they co-construct pedagogical theories and practices for teachers that are socially, culturally, and critically relevant for their daily lives and social futures. Kelly's research acknowledges the absence of youth voice in the process of educational design and as result she is embarking on a project that will highlight how youth develop pedagogical theories and identities. When engaging with hip-hop, primarily within educational spaces, there must be an acknowledgment of youth voice and perceptions. Dr. Kelly's work can serve as an exemplar for educators across the nation on how to leverage youth voice to create pedagogies and instructional materials that are authentic to the multiples identities that youth embody.

To learn more about Dr. Lauren Leigh Kelly's research and scholarship, check out the following:

- Kelly, L. L. (2020). "I am not Jasmine; I am Aladdin": How youth challenge structural inequity through critical hip hop literacies. *International Journal of Critical Media Literacy, 1*(2), 9–30. https://doi.org/10.1163/25900110-00201002.
- Kelly, L. L. (2020). Listening differently: Youth self-actualization through critical hip hop literacies. *English Teaching: Practice & Critique, 19*(3), 269–285.
- Kelly, L. L. (2019). Building critical classroom community through hip-hop literature. *The English Journal, 109*(1), 52–58.
- Kelly, L. L., & Sawyer, D. C. (2019). "When keeping it real goes wrong": Enacting critical pedagogies of hip-hop in mainstream schools. *IASPM Journal, 9*(2), 6–21.
- Kelly, L. L. (2016). "You don't have to claim her": Reconstructing Black femininity through critical hip-hop literacy. *Journal of Adolescent & Adult Literacy, 59*(5), 529–538. (Included in Vol. 51 2016 "Annotated Bibliography of Research in the Teaching of English.")
- Kelly, L. L. (2013). Hip-Hop literature: The politics, poetics, and power of hip-hop in the English classroom. *English Journal, 102*(5), 50–55.

References

Freire, P. (2012). *Pedagogy of the oppressed*. Rowman & Littlefield.
Greene, M. (1988). *Dialectic of freedom*. Teachers College Press.
Love, B. L. (2016). Complex personhood of hip hop & the sensibilities of the culture that fosters knowledge of self & self-determination. *Equity & Excellence in Education, 49*(4), 414–427.
Thompson, H. A. (2011). Criminalizing kids: The overlooked reason for failing schools. *Dissent, 58*(4), 23–27.

· 7 ·

ON AUTHENTICITY FROM A STUDENT AND TEACHER PERSPECTIVE: KEEPING IT REAL WITH VICTORIA RICHARDSON

Victoria Richardson is a New York City public school educator who identifies as a writer, poet, daughter, and sneakerhead. Victoria had the unique experience of engaging with hip-hop in her high school science class through the Science Genius program in 2013. She went on to be a Science Genius finalist and had the opportunity to showcase her science-themed song for educators and community members at Teachers College, Columbia University. Victoria's experiences in K-12 education encouraged her to pursue her Master of Education at Teachers College, Columbia University, and ultimately return to her middle school to serve as a teacher. In this chapter, Victoria provides insight into the importance of authenticity, hip-hop, and teaching.

Edmund:	Wassup Victoria! Tell us who you are and how you identify yourself.
Victoria Richardson:	I'm Victoria Richardson. I'm a teacher and educator. I'm a writer. I'm a girl who wears hats.
Edmund:	Can you share your experiences as a New York City public school student?
Victoria Richardson:	When I was younger, I was many different types of student. It depends on what timeframe we're looking at. I was a student, and there were times in my life when I was a student who was on point and a "teacher's pet." I answered all the questions. I

	was well-behaved. I shut up when it was time to shut up, talking when it was time to talk. Then I hit middle school, and it was a transformation for me. I was not that kid anymore. I was the kid challenging my teachers and playing devil's advocate all the time. I think that was the time when I was figuring out who I was and what it meant to be a Black girl, and what it meant to have this kind of freedom that you get in middle school and have an opinion that I feel matters after being silenced for so long. That student was very talkative, very opinionated, very matter-of-fact, challenged authority, and was very authentic.
Edmund:	You talk about being a docile and compliant student in elementary school, and then there was a shift in middle school. You mentioned exploring your Black girl identity. Is there anything more to that? What do you think caused that shift?
Victoria Richardson:	When I got older, I was exposed to more. I understood things a little bit differently. I don't know that time period, but it was at the beginning of Nicki Minaj's career. I was seeing people be themselves, and in the elementary school that I attended, students were docile and quiet. When I went to middle school, it was different. People were themselves. I guess that kind of gave me the invitation to also be me. I'm not saying there was a realization that I was like, "Hey, like I'm a black girl, whoa." But it was different; I just had more knowledge and life experience at that point.
Edmund:	Okay. How did Nicki Minaj impact that? You said you related to her. What about her?
Victoria Richardson:	I was never a Nicki fan. Let's put that out there. But she was on the TV screen, and a lot of the time, there wasn't anybody else who looked like her who was on the TV screen, who was rapping, or who was just being their authentic self. Nicki was opinionated, she was loud, and she was ratchet. She was talking with her hands. She was doing all that stuff that, you know, feels natural or feels like—represents how I want to be or how I feel like I am compared to seeing other softer, quieter R&B artists. A lot of people were also emulating Nicki at that time. A lot of the girls in my school were acting like her, and we would walk around singing her songs and doing all the ra-ra (gestures), like the monster song and all of that.
Edmund:	That's dope. So, what aspects of schooling or relationships with teachers didn't you appreciate or didn't spark your interest?
Victoria Richardson:	I think I learned in school that there's one way that you're supposed to be, there's one way that you're supposed to act, there's one way that you're supposed to speak, there's one way that you're supposed to conduct yourself and that was very confining

for me. Now, I've been through college and indoctrinated, so now my language is a little bit different from how it was when I was in K-12 schools, but I speak colloquially. A lot of the times—or I would say like," Oh, that ain't right," or like, the teacher would mark on the paper, *"not proper English."* I could have demonstrated my understanding of the question but would not get it right because of how I answered it. Or in other ways, like, I was always too loud for this, or I was—and it sounds really cliche, but it was things that I dealt with. Just having teachers that didn't understand me and the way that I engaged in the world led to a cultural mismatch. I will never forget these experiences. And it's crazy because I kind of relive it every day because of where I work.

Victoria reflects on her experiences as a New York City public school student and recalls being docile and compliant during elementary school. She followed orders from her teachers without question. She spoke when it was time to talk, and when it was time to be quiet, she was quiet. In our patriarchal society, Black girls are often encouraged to follow the rules without question, or they risk being labeled a "Bad" girl, a "ghetto" girl, or even ratchet (Morris, 2016). Nikki Jones posits, "good girls do not look or act like men or boys. Good girls do not run wild in the streets; instead, they spend most of their time in a controlled setting: family, school, home, or church" (Jones, 2006). Through these controlled spaces, Black girls are conditioned to think and act according to patriarchal values. Victoria learned that schools taught her that there was only one way to exist—obedience. But as Victoria got older (middle school), she gained increased exposure to the world, which supported her in developing her understanding of the world and her identities. This new understanding of the world encouraged Victoria to explore her Black girl identity. Victoria saw representations of Black women who engaged in the world as their authentic selves, like Nicki Minaj, which gave her the invitation to present as her authentic self and lean into her ratchet identity. In his book Ratchetdemic, Emdin (2021) offers a conceptualization of the ratchet identity. Emdin shares, "we all got some ratchet in us. In other words, everyone has a piece of who they are that they are forced to hide for the sake of acceptance. The issue is that some folks have to hide their identity while others can express themselves more freely" (p. 68). Further, Emdin shares that individuals who actualize a ratchet identity "[reach] the point when one becomes a weapon, one unearths a tool that helps one to shape one's own identity and define oneself for who one truly is" (p. 68). Seeing Black women represented in media engage as their authentic selves encouraged Victoria to actualize her ratchet identity in middle school, as she began to feel comfortable in presenting her authentic self.

Edmund: So when you think about your experiences in schools, how did your experiences in schools impact your relationship with hip-hop and vice versa?

Victoria Richardson: Okay. So it wasn't until this, this conversation, or when I was reading the interview questions that I realized I actually did have a lot of hip-hop in my schooling. I was introduced to J. Cole, who is my favorite artist ever, through an ELA teacher who gave us the song *Lost Ones* in ninth grade. The teacher used the song to teach some type of literary device, and that really stuck with me because J. Cole was a great artist, and I had never even listened to him before. So that was something I think was really meaningful. In middle school, we did things like, we went to the hip-hop museum. There was a hip-hop museum or exhibit in Harlem at some point. It's not there anymore, I don't believe. But we went to this hip-hop museum on a field trip, we did graffiti, and we made this huge mural that I still have to this day. We learned about DJing and scratching and all of that stuff. We learned about all the five elements of hip-hop, which was really dope. But that same school that took us to the hip-hop museum was the same school that was policing the way we talked, the way we dressed, the way we acted—it was this big contradiction. So I guess back then, I didn't realize it was hip-hop education because you're taking me to a hip-hop museum. Okay, cool....but you're not practicing hip-hop practices, and you're not taking what hip-hop teaches us and using it in your school. You're just putting hip-hop there to say that we did hip-hop. Same thing with the teacher who used J. Cole in that lesson, right? It was dope. He put me onto J. Cole. But this was the same teacher who clearly had a racial bias and who clearly came to the school on some white savior crap. So that was a big contradiction.

And then there was Science Genius. I think that, for one, hip-hop really made science more enjoyable for that time period and also helped me remember stuff. I can name all the base pairs because of my science genius song. And that was like 10 years ago. I don't think I would have remembered such information if I had not—I can name the whole digestive system! I wouldn't have been able to do that. And I understand it!

Victoria's experiences with hip-hop in school signal the need for rigorous interpretations of hip-hop education. Emdin and Adjapong (2018) noted that hip-hop education is not just a fun thing that is done with kids in schools. Instead, hip-hop education "thrives on synthesis" and "promotes creativity and freedom of expression" (Emdin & Adjapong, 2018, p. 2). Ultimately, hip-hop education requires an immense amount of rigor and engagement (Emdin & Adjapong, 2018). What this rigor and engagement look like, however, is endless. While Victoria's experience in the Science Genius showcased rigor and engagement through the construction of raps, there is potential for a strategy like lyrical analysis—which Victoria's other teacher attempted—to be rigorous and engaging. We see rigorous and engaging lyrical analysis demonstrated by Stovall (2006), who utilized hip-hop lyrics to engage students in a critical conversation about lived experiences and systemic oppression. Bolstered by other sources that discussed the topics revealed in the hip-hop lyrics, Stovall (2006) centered lyrical analysis as a way to critically challenge the narratives in hip-hop music and provide space for students to reflect on the societal concerns they have. Imperative in implementing rigorous and engaging interpretations of hip-hop education is not only the broad understanding of the themes within hip-hop music and culture but also the belief that the themes in hip-hop are worthy of academic examination.

Kelly Allen: I think it is interesting that you recognized it as a contradiction in your in-school experiences, right? As you talked about that contradictory experience, I noticed you were like, "I remember the J. Cole song, but I don't remember what he was trying to teach me." Whereas, like with what you were just talking about with Science Genius, you're like, "I can remember science content." What do you think made those two experiences so different to the point where there was only one of the experiences that actually resulted in you saying, "I actually remember stuff because of this learning experience."

Victoria Richardson: Well, it's a couple of things. One was Science Genius is something that I did, that I created. I was making the product versus the product being given to me. Even though I love J. Cole and, you know, he's my man, it was different when I created my science-themed song. That's probably why I remember it so much deeper. And also because it required a different level of rigor to get there. It was a lot harder. I'm pretty sure the J. Cole lesson didn't require as much brain power. It was cool, but it wasn't rigorous compared to Science Genius, where I had to write a whole song about this thing that I know nothing about, which required a lot of productive struggle. Two, also the people who taught me, honestly. Through Science Genius, I ended up developing a really good relationship with my instructors, as opposed to my high school English teacher, who was a person whose class I dreaded to go into.

Edmund: What were your initial thoughts about teachers using hip-hop in school?

Victoria Richardson: Depends on which time. For example, with the J. Cole lesson, at first, I was like, who is this white man putting this rap song in front of me, blah, blah, blah. And, you know, I started with that, but I ended up loving J. Cole. I can't emphasize that enough. But then with Science Genius, it was also kind of the same thing almost, but not really because it's like, okay, they want us to learn science through hip-hop. They want me to rap. I'm in this little "I think I'm a rapper" phase anyway. Okay, let's do it!

But, this goes back to, like, who's presenting the information and your relationship with that person. I didn't know Chris Emdin from a hole in the wall, I didn't know these people with the cameras in my face from a hole in the wall, but the idea—I gave into it. I leaned into it because of how it was presented, because of the confidence of the person who was presenting it, and the knowledge. I could tell that these people, like Chris, knew hip-hop. They were really confident that this was going to work. Compared to, like I said, back to this other example of like the J. Cole lesson. Like at first, I'm like, I didn't know J. Cole. I know this white man is putting this rap song in my face, so I don't like him. And what are you doing? I ended up liking it, but my initial reaction was way different.

Edmund: You talked about the authenticity of teachers. Do you think that they were authentic when you have positive experiences with hip-hop in schools?

Victoria Richardson: That was the key difference between the teacher from high school who was just doing it because he's like, "oh, these Black kids like hip-hop, so let me give them hip-hop." I don't know, maybe he loved J. Cole. Perhaps he loved this song, but it didn't feel like that then especially because we didn't have that relationship, right? I didn't know anything about him. You don't have a Black card yet, so why are you coming up here with this hip-hop song trying to buy me in? That's what it felt like. Like I was being bought in because it's hip-hop, "It's black kids, put it together. Yeah, they love it!" Compared to like, it felt like there was passion, there was realness when it was introduced through the Science Genius program.

I guess because it just with Science Genius, they were actually interested in hip-hop, and they weren't doing it for the sake of teaching it. They were leaning into the part of hip-hop or the place in hip-hop that resonated with them. Like say, if that teacher from my high school really loved hip-hop, and that showed throughout his whole presentation since the day I met him—you know, if I saw him walking around listening to hip-hop, if he showed his personality beforehand—it would've seemed less random.

The teacher that used J. Cole didn't show that it was authentic, and I think it has to be real to you. If you don't like rap music, then don't use rap music in your lesson. There's another way, you know? There are other connections that can be made because it's not gonna hit if it's not authentic. And it's not going to present authenticity. You can't fake authenticity. That's the point.

I mean, we're always open to people learning. In that case, if I wanted to use hip-hop in my lesson, I would use the experts, which would be my students. So that would be a perfect place to: "this is what I'm learning, you already know a lot more about it. How can we use this? How can we come together to teach a lesson about this using this"

Edmund: Right. Do you know who you remind me of Victoria when you talk about the teacher, the white teacher who taught the J. Cole lesson? You remind me of the teacher who's like, "Yo, we're gonna do this really dope thing centered around hip-hop tomorrow" it gets everybody super excited, they do the dope thing, the kids have a good time, and then that dope thing never finds its way back in the classroom ever again. What's the point of leveraging students' culture only once if it's not going to be a permanent fixture in the classroom?

Victoria Richardson: And they drop it.

Edmund: Why can't we have those positive experiences more frequently, or even daily, within our learning experiences? That is what you have me thinking about.

Victoria Richardson: That's true.

Kelly Allen: Yeah. Yeah. It's like, it's just like this, like a one-off "pedagogical tool."

Victoria Richardson: A tool, right.

Kelly Allen: It's deeper than that, right? Just thrown in there, like, "Eh, okay."

Edmund: It demonstrates that it's literally used as a hook, right?

Victoria Richardson: Yes

Kelly Allen: Yeah.

Edmund:	It shows they use people's culture as only a hook.
Victoria Richardson:	And you know why I think they do that? It's because it requires a lot of preparation. If I'm not an expert in this already, I have to do a lot of learning before I can do this. So I have to learn about this thing, and I have to learn about this thing, and I have to put it together to teach you about it.

Victoria's experience as a student demonstrates the reality that the work of hip-hop education doesn't start the moment you bring hip-hop into the classroom. Even more, it sends oppressive messages to students if you approach hip-hop education this way. Victoria's experience with feeling as if hip-hop was positioned as a pedagogical tool is articulated by Evans, Allen and Turner (2020) when they state,

> The concept of the hook—which includes motivational energy and linking content to students' lives to create pathways to new information—has been indoctrinated by teacher education programs, leading teachers to believe that a hook is the first step in expanding students' minds to the curricular topics that follow (Gonzalez, 2014). I have questioned whether the practice of hooking students into engaging with a lesson is compatible with culturally responsive frameworks (Gay, 2002; Ladson Billings, 1994) or if using a lesson hook is a method of tapping into students' cultures to entice, befriending, or lull young minds into a slumber of preconceived units of learning. We argue the latter. Through employing the hook, student culture and culturally responsive pedagogy are often misappropriated in ways that hoodwink students into engaging with their teacher and the learning process. (p. 57)

Victoria's teacher's attempt to incorporate hip-hop into the curriculum was unsuccessful, even though Victoria identified hip-hop music as an integral part of her culture, partly because it was positioned as a one-off strategy to hook students into learning. This phenomenon is reminiscent of the way the commercialization of hip-hop has packed the culture of hip-hop youth to sell it for profit, in the sense that teachers are "using" hip-hop culture to entice students to "buy in" to academic standards they have set (Emdin & Adjapong, 2018). The attempted implementation of hip-hop education by Victoria's teacher also speaks to the need for authenticity in this work. No curriculum or pedagogical strategy can outweigh white supremacists' deficit perspectives of students and their community.

Edmund:	You talked about the challenges of your experiences with hip-hop in education. Is there anything else you want to say about that?

Victoria Richardson: I think something that I think has been challenged from the teacher's perspective is that not every kid is going to connect with hip-hop in the same way. So, you're not always going to reach every kid with every hip-hop lesson. It's not like a thing that you can just use and every kid will be engaged. Some kids don't like hip-hop, and they don't like anything related to hip-hop. Some don't know what it is. It wasn't until I was an adult that I began to understand more about hip-hop. So a lot of students don't know, and you might—there have been times that I've used certain things as like a way to increase engagement, and I'm like "that didn't actually work". I think a challenge is, one, you have to really know your students, and you have to really know what they know and what they care about—and how it relates to your content. Then figure out how it relates to hip-hop. Finally, figure out how you can use that in the classroom.

Victoria highlights that not every student will connect to the use of hip-hop within educational spaces, which is correct. Victoria also recognizes that when she got older and as an adult, she was able to learn and understand hip-hop more. Young people currently have little to no opportunity to engage, interrogate, and explore hip-hop culture within schools. Youth are often consumed with commercialized versions of hip-hop culture, which can be misleading if not interrogated through a critical lens. It is the educators' responsibility to create the context for hip-hop to emerge in the classroom, but this should be done with and through how students experience, appreciate, and engage with hip-hop. This requires educators to have an authentic understanding of their students before they can incorporate hip-hop in a meaningful way.

Edmund: What would you envision if you could radically dream about the future of hip-hop in education?

Victoria Richardson: I think we wouldn't have spaces that are using hip-hop as a hook but then not practicing the values of hip-hop, not respecting the culture that hip-hop lives out of. Not having schools that want to use hip-hop and take us on hip-hop trips and all of these things, but then don't value the culture, the people, or the cultural practices that come out of hip-hop or the people who started hip-hop have. I feel like those things can't coexist.

Victoria's radical dream for the field of hip-hop and education is for educators and educational institutions to authentically engage in hip-hop. Victoria has not always experienced authentic representations of hip-hop culture within educational spaces and highlights that inauthentic hip-hop practice demonstrates a lack of appreciation and value of hip-hop culture. Often schools and teachers utilize hip-hop as a hook or solely for engagement rather than find ways to entirely and authentically incorporate hip-hop and its sensibilities. When we focus on hip-hop as a hook in schools, were are not utilizing its full potential, and the very youth whom schools are looking to engage may see through the inauthentic variation of hip-hop. With the support of educational research, and countless curricular and pedagogical exemplars of critical and authentic hip-hop education, we should continue to dream about the limitless possibilities of the authentic incorporation of hip-hop within educational spaces.

References

Emdin, C., & Adjapong, E. (2018). #HipHopEd: The compilation on hip hop education: Volume 1: Hip-Hop as education, philosophy, and practice. Boston: Brill Sense.

Stovall, D. (2006). We can relate: Hip-Hop culture, critical pedagogy, and the secondary classroom. *Urban Education, 41*(6), 585–602. https://doi.org/10.1177/0042085906292513.

Jones, N. (2009). *Between good and ghetto: African American girls and inner-city violence*. Rutgers University Press.

· 8 ·

THE POWER OF HIP-HOP AS A TOOL: KEEPING IT REAL WITH CHRISTOPHER EMDIN

Dr. Christopher Emdin is the Robert A. Naslund Endowed Chair in Curriculum Theory and Professor of Education at the University of Southern California, where he also serves as the Director of youth engagement and community partnerships at the USC Race and Equity Center. Dr. Emdin is the creator of the #HipHopEd social media movement, a non-profit organization that aims to empower communities and reimagine the relationship between hip-hop and education. He is also the author of many award-winning books, including *Urban Science Education for the Hip-Hop Generation*, *For White Folks Who Teach In the Hood and the Rest of Ya'll too*, *Ratchetdemic: Reimagining Academic Success* and *STEM, STEAM, Make, Dream*.

Edmund: Can you explain how you identify yourself as a scholar?
Dr. Chris Emdin: I see myself as a scholar-practitioner. I don't believe that the concept of scholarship can be teased away from doing work that has a direct impact on communities and young people. I appreciate what scholarship means within the construct of academia and how that infrastructure is built, but I also see the limitations of a more traditional perception of a scholar. I think that identifying as a hip-hop scholar recognizes that it has to be equal parts intellectual and practical, it has to be theoretical and tangible, and even when I'm doing intellectual and philosophical work, I always construct those

	ideas with an idea in the back of my mind about how both ideas will be perceived and interpreted by people. I'm a scholar-practitioner with deep philosophical roots that believes in the concept of practical application. I think that scholarship becomes scholar-shit if it doesn't speak directly to the people
Edmund:	What groups do you primarily consider in your work and research?
Dr. Chris Emdin:	I write to teachers, but for students. It's an exciting way of looking at it. The direct audience who will be reading the work are teachers, aspiring teachers, or people who work in the field of education. So, I'm intentional about who is receiving it. It's to educators, but it's for the children. So, when I write, I'm not writing to appease the population that it's to. I'm writing to them for young folks.

I sometimes don't have control over who picks up my work, but I know no matter who picks it up, they will read it and know it's for the babies. The work is for urban, marginalized youth, those who have a tendency to engage in and with hip-hop culture, and those who have been written off by traditional school systems. The tools can change, but the force will not. |

Dr. Christopher Emdin aims to produce work that will impact urban and marginalized youth. While Emdin acknowledges that youth may not consume his research, his hope is that the educators and administrators who engage with his work will see and hear their students through it. Because of his focus on youth, even though he often takes a philosophical approach to scholarship, his goal is to make the philosophical practical. Therefore, he aims to make his work tangible and practical for individuals that work directly with youth.

Edmund:	So, hip-hop is a tool for you. You embody hip-hop, and you identify as hip-hop. In terms of your pedagogy, your scholarship, and the way you engage in the world, you're bringing a part of your personal self into that space.
Dr. Chris Emdin:	Absolutely. And as a tool it's a piece of my identity, and it's also a tool that I've been able to use to navigate. And like any tool, the power of the tool is only fully understood when you know how to use it. You've got a powerful tool without the ability to understand how to use it. You could actually destroy your project. If I've got a hammer and I don't know how to use it, I might smash my finger and be in pain—or worse, inflict pain onto someone else. You have to understand the nature of the tool. You have to understand when to use the hammer. So hip-hop is a tool, but with that tool comes a set of instructions and responsibilities about how to use the tool appropriately.

Emdin identifies hip-hop as a tool that can be leveraged within educational spaces to create opportunities for liberation. He acknowledges that he personally identifies as part of hip-hop, which offers him a unique vantage point and perspective on the utilization of hip-hop across educational spaces. When we consider hip-hop as a culture created to counter oppressive systems and structures and create opportunities for joy and liberation for those who have been systemically marginalized, it may feel reductive to consider hip-hop as a tool. However, as Dr. Emdin reminds us, in the conceptualization of hip-hop as a tool, we cannot disregard the instructions and responsibilities that come along with the tool. To this end, we are reminded of our discussion in chapter one with Gloria Ladson-Billings and her recognition that what she originally conceptualized as culturally relevant pedagogy has often become unrecognizable through the implementation of educators. Too often, culturally engaged pedagogies have been reduced to a set of pedagogical strategies that teachers can pick up and put down at will. As a culturally engaged pedagogy, the same can be said of hip-hop. Therefore, in positioning hip-hop as a tool, the understanding that culturally engaged pedagogies like hip-hop education are "only as important as the ideas behind [them] and the enactments it engenders," is imperative (Paris & Alim, 2017, p. 13). Thus, without a recognition that no attempt for liberation can be successful if the educator pursuing liberation does not recognize the oppression that students are experiencing, and the role they play in perpetuating students' oppression, there is a risk of misappropriating hip-hop education and perpetuating oppression.

Engaging in hip-hop education as a liberatory praxis requires more than a simple incorporation of hip-hop; it also requires educators to understand the responsibility they hold to engage in hip-hop education through a critical perspective. Emdin explains that utilizing hip-hop within educational spaces requires critical perspectives and an understanding of the intention and necessity of hip-hop. To support educators in developing critical perspectives as it relates to the use of hip-hop within educational spaces, we encourage all educators, regardless of experience with hip-hop, to interrogate their positionality (Adjapong & Allen, 2023) in relation to hip-hop culture and the students who will receive hip-hop informed instruction. Through this examination of self, educators must recognize that they cannot utilize hip-hop to be "cool" or for self-gratification. The use of hip-hop within educational spaces should support liberation and joy, particularly for groups who have experienced systemic oppression.

Edmund:	In your personal opinion and experience in working with hip-hop and teachers, what skills and understandings do you think educators need to effectively leverage hip-hop as a practice?
Dr. Chris Emdin:	The first thing has to be doing some kind of personal work around their relationship to hip-hop. When was the first time you listened to any hip-hop at all? What's your favorite song? What's a recent song? Literally just utilizing their own self-interrogation of their relationship to the cultures and music of the artifacts as a springboard to what you do next in the classroom.

What you'll find when you do that kind of work is, "Oh, so your favorite song is a song by Too $hort that goes 'Bitch, that's my favorite word.'" Like, that's your favorite song? Word. Let's talk about why that's the case. Is it just because of how it sounds? So I think utilizing relationships to or experiences with hip-hop as an opening point to do some interrogation of self is a good preamble.

The second one would have to be just redefining what the purpose of teaching is. You can't do the hip-hop work if you don't understand why we teach. Do you teach to deliver content, for engagement, or motivation? Like, you've got to know what the goals of teaching are because if you tell me goals that are anti hip-hop or anti what I think education is it's just going to ruin it. It's going to be a negative experience for you, it's going to be a negative experience for kids. Like, if you want to use hip-hop to help you pass your next test. Do you think a test is the ultimate goal? If you think that, then don't use hip-hop. Just keep doing all the same trash you've been doing. |
Edmund:	Yeah.
Dr. Chris Emdin:	I also think that because hip-hop music is such a prevalent dimension of the culture, seeing the manifestation of hip-hop through other avenues is going to be really important. What I mean by that is the intersections of hip-hop in other areas of study. Not even just the elements. Like what has hip-hop done to social media? You know, what has hip-hop done to architecture? What has hip-hop done to the arts?
Edmund:	Arts, theater, all that.
Dr. Chris Emdin:	Theater, right. So I think showcasing the ways that hip-hop has been able to permeate existing fields and improve the conditions, the products and the productivity of folks in those fields and saying, "Look at the growth in these arenas. Would you like to see that same growth in the classroom?" And that gives another avenue in to justify the use of the culture in a way that's transformative for young people.

Edmund:	I love your articulation. This reminds me of your articulation of hip-hop as a tool. So in order to use any tool you need to know what the tool does, how to use it effectively, how it could harm you possibly. So there's pre-work before you can pick up that tool.
Dr. Chris Emdin:	Absolutely!
Edmund:	So this is the pre-work for teachers and hopefully that pre-work will support them in the work that they're doing while they're teaching and engaging. I think in order to engage in hip-hop as an educator, like you said, you have to push through the tropes that we have of hip-hop and even more importantly we have to push through the tropes that we have of Blackness. Hip-Hop is a Black culture and that's where we've got to start. So if you have any uncomfortability around Blackness, we have to explore that before we can talk about hip-hop which is a Black culture.
Dr. Chris Emdin:	I couldn't have said that any better.

Emdin posits that without doing the "personal work" of understanding your own relationship to and with hip-hop culture and Blackness, it will be impossible to critically engage in hip-hop education. This sentiment is echoed by others in the book as well. In chapter four, Dr. David Stovall noted that educators engaging in hip-hop education must do "the inward facing work" to avoid the misappropriation of hip-hop culture. We see the effect of not doing this "inward facing work" in chapter seven when Victoria described her experience learning from an educator who didn't appear to deeply engage with hip-hop culture when attempting to engage in hip-hop education. As a result, the teacher's attempts at including hip-hop into the curriculum came across as inauthentic. This experience informed Victoria's freedom dream for hip-hop education, which envisioned a future where educators and scholars authentically engage in hip-hop education.

If we are to realize Victoria's freedom dream that educators and scholars authentically engage in hip-hop education, there has to be a critical engagement with doing "inward facing" or "personal work", to quote Dr. Stovall and Dr. Emdin. One way to begin this work is by engaging with the Framework for Hip-Hop Educator and Researcher Positionality (Adjapong & Allen, 2023). Though we mentioned this briefly in the discussion of Dr. Stovall's concerns of misappropriation in chapter four, we wanted to expand on our conceptualization of the Framework for Hip-Hop Educator and Researcher Positionality here. A full overview of the framework can be found in Table 8.1. In our conceptualization of the Framework for Hip-Hop Educator and Researcher Positionality, we state,

"We have found that a lack of interrogation of whiteness and positionality while engaging in hip-hop based education and research can contribute to a replication of the same systemic inequities that the field and study of hip-hop education are working towards eradicating. In addition, most educators and researchers who engage in hip-hop based education superficially leverage hip-hop to maintain the status quo as opposed to creating educational spaces where students are able to critique hip-hop culture as well as systems and structures that contribute to the collective oppression of historically marginalized groups (Turner, Allen & Evans, 2020). Further, scholars have used hip-hop within educational spaces to police how and what aspects of hip-hop culture and sensibilities enter the classroom spaces (Ender, 2021). We reject the incorporation of hip-hop into schooling and research only to the extent that it fits comfortably within the confines of white norms and values that permeate schooling (Ladson-Billings, 2013)." (Adjapong & Allen, 2023, p. 18).

Table 8.1. The Framework for Hip-Hop Educator and Researcher Positionality

Framework Tenet	Description of Tenet	Guiding Questions
Researching the Self	*Hip-Hop educators and researchers must engage in a critical reflection of themself, which must include a reflection of their ideologies, beliefs, and practices in relation to the hip-hop population they are engaged with as well as the Black communities that create hip-hop.*	What is my understanding of hip-hop history as it relates to my research or school context? What is my experience with hip-hop culture? How do these experiences inform my teaching and research? In what ways does my racial and cultural background influence the way I engage with hip-hop culture? What do I believe about hip-hop culture? How do I negotiate my beliefs about hip-hop culture in my teaching and research? How do I know? How do I negotiate and balance my racial and cultural selves as it relates to hip-hop and in my research? How do I know? What racialized and cultural experiences have shaped my research decisions, practices, approaches, epistemologies, and agendas?

Framework Tenet	Description of Tenet	Guiding Questions
Researching the Self in Relation to Others	*Hip-Hop educators and researchers must examine themselves in relation to the hip-hop populations they are working with. This examination must center on the Black communities that created hip-hop.*	What cultural and historical connections does the hip-hop population I am working with have to hip-hop? How do these connections influence the way the hip-hop populations interact with me, my teaching, and my research?
		What beliefs do the hip-hop populations that I am working with have about hip-hop, and how are these beliefs shaped by their racialized and cultural lived experiences?
		How do I negotiate and balance my own beliefs and interests around hip-hop with those of hip-hop populations I am engaged with, even if they are inconsistent with or diverge from mine?
Engaged Reflection and Representation	*Hip-Hop educators and researchers must acknowledge and represent the voices and perspectives of the hip-hop populations they are engaged with, regardless of their alignment with the perspectives of the educator or researcher.*	Educators and researchers should ask students:
		• How do you engage in hip-hop culture (MC, breakdancing, graffiti, DJ, knowledge of self)? How do you envision these aspects of hip-hop culture interacting with our classroom community?
		Educators and researchers should ask themselves:
		• How can you authentically incorporate students' understandings and relationships to hip-hop in your classroom/research?
• What would it look like to authentically incorporate students' understandings and relationships to hip-hop in your classroom/research?

Framework Tenet	Description of Tenet	Guiding Questions
		Researchers should discuss findings with the hip-hop populations engaged in the research.
		Teachers should discuss pedagogical and curricular implementations of hip-hop with students after the learning experience to understand what went well and what should be modified in the future.
Shifting From Self to System	*Hip-Hop educators and researchers must position themselves and their participants within the broader social, historical and political contexts that hip-hop culture, education, pedagogy, and research reside.*	What is the contextual nature of hip-hop in this study/praxis? What does hip-hop mean to the hip-hop populations involved in this work?
		What is known historically, socially, culturally, and racially about the hip-hop populations involved in this work?
		What barriers and structures—particularly ones that are systemic, institutionalized, or localized—influence the experiences that the hip-hop population I am working with has with hip-hop?
		How can I draw connections between curricular content and hip-hop praxis to interrogate institutional systems and structures that oppress specific groups?
		How can I leverage hip-hop research/praxis to interrogate institutional systems and structures that oppress specific groups?

*Table adapted from Adjapong and Allen (2023). For White Folks Who Teach Hip-Hop in Schools: Interrogating the Positionality of Hip-Hop Educators.

Our intent in conceptualizing this framework is that all educators and researchers who engage in hip-hop education—regardless of race or connectedness to/with hip-hop culture—have a sustained opportunity to interrogate their positionality.

Edmund:	What are your thoughts on folks expressing the need for more empirical research in the field of hip-hop and education?
Dr. Chris Emdin:	My take is that if you decide to engage in empirical research through hip-hop, so be it, but there has to concurrently be a recognition that because it's hip-hop, it doesn't have to be validated and that utilizing more empirical approaches or more traditional approaches does not by any means validate the power of hip-hop scholarship or the work of hip-hop scholarship, it's just another dimension of it.
	I think we have a tendency to attribute those characteristics of academic research as what makes it worth reading or what makes it necessary for those folks to get it. But here's the thing, our responsibility as hip-hop scholars is experiential and personal, and you've got to learn to understand the value of the personal and the experiential. If you don't have that in your relationship to hip-hop, you need to go find that. You need to get that. You need to go construct experiences for yourself that allows you to be able to feel the things I'm feeling.
	I'm not saying that more empirical and traditional research approaches should not be used at all. I'm just saying it should not be the gold standard. It should not be the benchmark. It should not be the requirement. I think when the work gets done with that, and it's fire? Oh, that's dope.
	At the same time, if somebody is like, "Yo, here's my personal experience working with hip-hop with these kids in this one classroom," we should be able to glean wisdom from that in the same way that we do more empirical studies. I think it's a perpetual conundrum that is rooted in the nature of academia.

Central to implementing hip-hop education is an understanding of the layers of oppression that exist in society and the belief that the social identities of students, teachers, and community members matter (Runell & Diaz, 2007). We argue that this understanding of oppression must extend to academic examinations of hip-hop education. Academia has long been criticized for its failure to adequately support faculty that produce critical scholarship (Bridget & Winkle-Wagner, 2017; Croom, 2017; Haynes et al., 2020; Turner & Allen, 2022). Emdin's assertion that hip-hop research does not need to be validated through traditional, empirical approaches is part of a larger history of conversations amongst critical academics about the oppression they face in academia, some of which are described throughout this book. For example, in chapter three, Dr. Thandi Hicks Harper discussed her pressure to embed her work in traditional, whitewashed methodologies and perspectives. The tension Dr. Hicks Harper felt was a result of her continual struggle to convince individuals that hip-hop is worthy of examination in academic spaces. As noted in the discussion of Dr. Hicks Harpers' experience, the reality that works on hip-hop education is continually seen as invalid in academic spaces unless it conforms to traditional, whitewashed approaches to research methodology and design is a result of pervasive anti-Blackness that has infected academia. In fact, Emdin (2018) argues that

> "much of the existing work in hip-hop and education still functions within a paradigm that is rooted in a desire for acceptance from those outside of the culture. We ask why the beauty, complexity, and brilliance of hip-hop lyrics have to be accepted by the same people and institutions that failed the young people who wrote them?" (p. 3)

While Emdin's (2018) quote was talking about the inclusion of hip-hop in K-12 spaces, we argue that this sentiment applies to academic examinations of hip-hop education as well. Because of the pressures of tenure and promotion for university professors, many hip-hop scholars are pressured to validate their research according to the standards set by academic institutions or opt to not fully engage in hip-hop informed scholarship. The issue is that institutional standards are rooted in whitewashed approaches to knowledge production that simply do not and cannot honor the brilliance and complexity of hip-hop culture. For example, while academic institutions privilege empirical research published in purported "top-tier" journals, hip-hop culture always has privileged communal knowledge that is spread through conversations at kickbacks, the hair salon or barber shop, or passed down through generations by elders. Therefore, it's necessary for hip-hop scholars to publish work that is reflective and highlights their personal experiences and tensions with the culture. Also, hip-hop scholars may opt to publish work that is more accessible for communities, teachers, and students engaged in hip-hop, even if the outlet for this work is not a "top-tier" journal. This sentiment is seen in how individuals throughout the book describe their approach to scholarship, their identity as a scholar, and what they hope their work achieves. Throughout the book, the academics featured have discussed the need for their work to be relevant and practical for students, teachers, and communities. The reality is that if a scholar is wanting teachers and community members to access their work, the best outlet may not be a "top-tier" journal that requires findings to be couched within dense empirical data and hidden behind a paywall. For hip-hop scholars, there is nothing "top-tier" about the communities and individuals who you hope to take up your work not being able to access your research.

However, the sharing of knowledge through more collaborative approaches is not always privileged by academic institutions. Despite academic institutions' attempted constraints on scholarly engagement, hip-hop scholars continue to grapple with how to effectively expand the work they do with teachers, students, and the community.

Edmund: If you could radically dream about the future of hip-hop in education, what would you envision?

Dr. Chris Emdin: You know, believe it or not, I think about this often. I think about institutions of higher education, they're so deeply entrenched into hip-hop sensibilities that it's impossible to be able to name them as outside of what being academic is. Could you imagine going to a place where it's like they get it so much that when I walk in to the first floor lobby, hip-hop is playing in the backdrop and I get into the class and there is hip-hop art on the walls and then I get a textbook for the semester and it's hip-hop themed? That it's so deeply entrenched into the fabric of the operation of the space that even saying, "Oh that's a hip-hop this," you'd be like, "What? Of course it is." In much the same way as a concept like cultural relevance or youth-centered or youth-focused is prescribed.

What would happen in an institution like that is that there would be a very dramatic reversal of who is seen and what is seen as valuable and not. So, folks who are not deeply entrenched in the culture will be at a deficiency. Then we'd have to showcase the kind of kindness that they have not shown to us in getting them onboard because hip-hop always does it better.

When I think about that, the normalizing of deep cultural truths, not in a way where it's adulterated or in a way that it's a fabrication of the truth, but authentic representations of the culture being the standard, is something I think about often.

Also, I can't do this without considering K-12. I often dream of school. That's what the work that we try to do is. If we Science Genius the curriculum, and then we Collider Classroom this space, now the curriculum and the space are aligned with young folks' sensibilities. Like, I can learn this way and feel good here. Like, imagine what would happen if that was the norm everywhere.

Edmund: Yeah. That's dope, man. One last thing you got me thinking about now is, you talk about if we leverage hip-hop in a lot of different educational spaces, then those who are intrinsically hip-hop will have to welcome those who aren't or don't identify as hip-hop. When you talk about hip-hop, a lot of the argument is that this is for Black and Brown kids, right? Because we know that white kids, white youth are the top consumer, the ones who are spending money on hip-hop. So I don't even know folks who want to believe that argument.

Dr. Chris Emdin: Bro, here's the argument that people aren't even considering. Across the globe, any population who has been historically marginalized or oppressed aligns themselves to hip-hop. Here's the thing, not just American hip-hop, their own. Like they construct their own hip-hop. What I'm saying is hip-hop has become the tool for healing for any population who's been decentered anywhere. So when I talk about hip-hop being normalized, what I'm essentially saying, utilizing hip-hop as a language, is that those who have been historically and traditionally marginalized and oppressed by systems of power become the ones that hold the power.

And yeah, hip-hop becomes the lens through which I describe that, but that's what the goal is, the ultimate goal is to have those most historically marginalized utilizing their own cultural artifacts as the tool through which they learn, engage, and gain access and power to whatever the world has to offer. That's the dream.

Edmund: That's it. And we're able to flip the power dynamics in that way.

Dr. Chris Emdin: Absolutely,. I think we'll get there because I'm a perpetual optimist. And when we get there, we will show those who did not give us the kind of love we deserved how to utilize the culture to bring love. Because that's what we've always done. We've always done that. When people talk about the power of Black women and all that, some folks take that concept and utilize it as a mechanism to demean and disempower. Those who know that it's about being able to see the redemptive possibility in the brokenness of a system or a world, or a population, that's the essence. I think that hip-hop manifests that because of its inclusive nature.

This is why South Koreans have created the most amazing hip-hop artists, and the Maori in New Zealand create the most amazing hip-hop because it showcases the way to find humanity in the midst of brokenness.

Edmund: Yeah. That's dope. That's a fact, I think. Hip-Hop is healing, hip-hop in a sense, is kind of saving the world.

Dr. Chris Emdin: Bro, hip-hop is the thing that can you get you out of your funk. Listen, when I'm feeling hated on, and I'm feeling frustrated and I feel like cats are trying to come for me, and I throw on Jay Rock's "Win", in five minutes, that leaves, and I'm like, good. It's a therapy tool, it's a mechanism to be able to overcome your brokenness, it's a pathway to a more expansive view of possibility in the midst of downtroddenness, and that's why we do #HipHopEd, because schools, the chief thing that contemporary schools manufacture is the downtroddenness of Black and Brown children.

Edmund:	And the cycle of that.
Dr. Chris Emdin:	And the cycle of it. The repetitive nature of it.
Edmund:	Yeah, exactly.
Dr. Chris Emdin:	Hip-Hop is the interrupter to that downtroddenness. That's why we keep using hip-hop, that's why we keep bringing it in.
Edmund:	That's the clear argument for hip-hop in educational spaces.
Dr. Chris Emdin:	Oppression is what it is. Hip-Hop is freedom.
Edmund:	It's a relationship.
Dr. Chris Emdin:	It's a relationship. It's a thing. It opens the door. It's light amid darkness. And the last thing I'll say on this is, for me, hip-hop is a contemporary manifestation of the power of Black music. What I'm talking about here really is Black music. Black music has always done that. I remember my pops, my pops if we have a long day, and he throws on some Fela-Kuti and I saw what it did to his spirit, it's Black music, Black music is the boom bap to storytelling, the cadence, the rhyme. Hip-Hop becomes a tool where all the complexities of Black music get packaged into a palatable artifact. Hip-Hop is the manifestation of all the complexities of Black music and its healing quality. That's why hip-hop.

To learn more about Dr. Christopher Emdin's research and scholarship, check out the following:

- Emdin, C., & Adjapong, E. (Eds.). (2018). #HipHopEd: The compilation on hip-hop education: Volume 1: Hip-Hop as education, philosophy, and practice. Brill.
- Emdin, C., & Lee, O. (2012). Hip-Hop, the "Obama effect," and urban science education. *Teachers College Record, 114*(2), 1–24.
- Emdin, C. (2010). Affiliation and alienation: Hip-Hop, rap, and urban science education. *Journal of Curriculum Studies, 42*(1), 1–25.

References

Adjapong, E., & Allen, K. R. (2023). For White folks who teach hip-hop—and the rest of Ya'll, too: Interrogating the positionality of hip-hop educators and researchers. *Equity & Excellence in Education*, 1–14. https://doi.org/10.1080/10665684.2023.2200208

Bridget, K., & Winkle-Wagner, R. (2017). Finding a voice in predominantly white institutions: A longitudinal study of Black women faculty members' journeys toward tenure. *Teachers College Record, 119*(6), 1–36.

Croom, N. N. (2017). Promotion beyond tenure: Unpacking racism and sexism in the experiences of Black womyn professors. *Review of Higher Education, 40*(4), 557–583.

Emdin, C. (2018). Introduction. In C. Emdin & E. Adjapong (Eds.), *#HipHopEd: The compilation on hip-hop education, volume 1: Hip-Hop as education, philosophy, and practice*. Brill Sense.

Haynes, C., Taylor, L., Mobley, S. D., & Haywood, J. (2020). Existing and resisting: The pedagogical realities of Black, critical men and women faculty. *Journal of Higher Education*, 91(5), 698–721.

Milner, H. R. (2007). Race, culture, and researcher positionality: Working through dangers seen, unseen, and unforeseen. *Educational Researcher*, 36(7), 388–400. https://www.jstor.org/stable/30136070

Runell, M., & Diaz, M. (2007). *The hip-hop education guidebook: Volume 1*. The Hip-Hop Association, Inc.

Turner, C. R., & Allen, K. R. (2022). *"She's a friend of my mind": A reflection of Black sisterhood in academia*. Race Ethnicity and Education.

· 9 ·

TOWARDS REALIZING FREEDOM DREAMS: REFLECTIONS AND NEXT STEPS

Edmund Adjapong: Let's start off with the intention for the book. I can share my intention for this book, which is to number one recognize and acknowledge how far hip-hop has come. Fifty years of a culture that is very intricate, complex, and nuanced and that centered around the uplifting of systemically marginalized groups and their voices. Hip-Hop offers opportunities for joy, freedom, and liberation to me, and that's what hip-hop is. This book is a celebration and acknowledgment of that. When we think about the celebration of hip-hop in the context of education, for me, it's a recognition that the field is still relatively new. There's a lot of brilliant and amazing work happening in the field of hip-hop and education, but we want to use this text as an opportunity to recenter our focus and be intentional about the work that we're doing and where we want the work to go. We want to be intentional about the impact and how this work manifests within educational spaces, manifests within educators, and, ultimately, how this work is manifesting with youth.

Kelly Allen: And I think, you know, building off of the intention of the work, for me as a new scholar, as I'm reading all this research and stuff, you begin to question, "What is my place in building upon this work?" And I think you often find yourself with more questions than answers. So the opportunity to dialogue with a lot of the OG's that have been writing about this, and just keeping it real with them, like "Yo, be honest with me. You wrote this, and be real with me: What did you mean by that? And what implications does that have for the field, and how do you envision the field building on what you were doing in a way that's going to actually be beneficial for hip-hop, for our communities, and for the field of hip-hop education?" And so, for me, ultimately, the intention was really just trying to wrap my head around what's next. Where do we as a field go from here?

Edmund Adjapong: What was your process in writing this book, and what were some insights, insights gained from it?

Kelly Allen: It was the dopest experience of my life since we are keeping it real! I think this whole project from the start to finish—from getting connected with you and starting to write about hip-hop education with you, all the way to doing all the interviews, all that kind of stuff—it really highlighted the importance of mentorship in this work. We have to be having more conversations with one another about the work that we're doing and how we're going about doing the work. Because for so long, I felt like I have been doing this work in isolation. I've been thinking about and engaging in hip-hop education for the last 10 years, but I've been doing it essentially by myself as a classroom teacher up until this last year or so. And even though I've been thinking about this work for the last 10 years, I feel like I learned more in this last year and a half collaborating with you and all of the people in the book than I have in the nine years before that. And I think a part of it is the way institutions operate. We are often siloed from one another in a lot of ways and we have to be really intentional about breaking down those walls, even the self-imposed ones. So yeah, I think I've learned a lot about myself as a scholar and as a person doing this work in schools and in my community, and what that work could look like.

Edmund Adjapong: Yeah, I get that. I think my intention was just to hear from folks doing this work for years. And just hear their perspectives and articulation of their work. You know, I agree with you. I think a lot of us do this work in isolation. It's important to give folks an opportunity to articulate their work. We can read papers, and we can do a meta-analysis, of course, right? But I think there's something powerful around hearing somebody share their intention or their desire behind something that they wrote or a concept that they were grappling with. The intention for this is to capture that. You know, I'm thinking about this book, like in a sense of a time capsule of sorts of where we are, and hopefully, we can look back at this book in 10, 15, or 20 years and be like—wow, that was a great opportunity and look how far we've come since that. So, I kind of want to, in some way, concretize the field and some of the highlights and conversations with some of the folks who have been doing the work for some time. Then using those perspectives to kind of put a call out to the field around this might be where we should be going next, or these are some considerations as we move forward in the field of hip-hop and education.

Throughout our conversations, there are many themes emerged. One theme is educators decentering themselves and also centering youth in relation to this work. What are your thoughts on that?

Kelly Allen: You know, I think this whole need for educators to decenter themselves and to recenter youth echoes the current state of education where teachers are constantly told through multiple different ways that they need to be the center of instruction. I think it also highlights how hip-hop, at its core, seeks to disrupt so much of the oppression youth are experiencing in schools. Part of that comes through recognizing that the intense focus on standardized instruction and the laws being passed right now that say what we can and can't teach, directly conflict with what hip-hop education aims to do. And so throughout this book, when we hear so many people talking about the need to recenter youth, I think we have to acknowledge that in this current state that we're in, that is a considerable act of resistance. It's no small thing.

Edmund Adjapong: Yeah. I would agree. I think that just I think hip-hop and education are polarizing ideas. I can recognize the challenge of like bringing them together, because I believe the essence of hip-hop is counter to traditional education and teaching, and learning. Within traditional education, teachers get a lot of messaging that they are the center, they are the sage on the stage. What we know creates effective teaching and effective learning environments when we center on those who are learning and when educators identify themselves as facilitators of knowledge. And I also think just encouraging educators to authentically understand their students' needs as opposed to assuming what they are that can be entrenched in bias.

Kelly Allen: Yeah, I hear that because when I talk about hip-hop education with the teachers that I work with they often say, "I love this idea of taking time to get to know who your students really are and centering them in instruction. That sounds great! But realistically, how do I do that because my district says I have to use this scripted curriculum and teach to all these standardized tests."

And I don't know what else to say to them, other than those things cannot coexist and any attempt at making them coexist is going to mean watering down what hip-hop education is meant to be. So, I don't know what else to say except for there has to be an intentional resistance to what the system is telling you to do when you know that it is not good for students. You gotta say "I'm rejecting that. I'm not buying into that. I'm not doing that. I'm refusing to teach that scripted curriculum. I refuse to teach to the test. I'm gonna close my door, and I'm gonna do what I know is best for students." And right now, there's a lot of consequences for teachers that do that. It's real out here right now. It's real. And I'm not trying to sugarcoat what doing the work actually looks like right now.

Edmund Adjapong: Yeah, absolutely. I think, yeah, we have to critically examine our school systems and structures. In order to do this, when we talk about hip-hop, hip-hop in education, is true reimagining of school systems. You know, and I don't know personally, how willing folks are, how willing how willing folks to do that. And also, some level the ability for folks to do that, you know,

Kelly Allen: I mean, you know, so much of what we're seeing occur right now is a manifestation of anti-Blackness in education, from the standardization of curriculum all the way to how we think we should interact with students. When you're working within a system that privileges anti-Blackness, and you are intentionally trying to disrupt anti-Blackness, racism, and oppression, it gets very real really quick.

Edmund Adjapong: It's problematic I mean, we are in a space where there are a lot of anti-black narratives that we are seeing in the state of Florida and across the whole country. It's evident. The youth know it and teachers are struggling to make sense of it. And we're creating all this controversy around thoughts and ideas that are not even leveraging K-12 schooling, like critical race theory. But the underpinning thought and idea are that we don't want the Black perspective taught in schools, we don't want to talk about oppression, and we don't want to talk about American history in schools. That trend is very detrimental to the Black and Brown students within schools, and at the same time, it continues to manifest this lack of understanding amongst those who do not understand the Black experience. So, it's detrimental to our society writ large.

Kelly Allen: Yeah, and I think it's easy right now for people to be like, "Oh, well, I don't agree with what Florida's doing, or I don't agree with the anti-CRT bans, so I'm not perpetuating anti-Blackness in education." We must recognize that you can see those blatant displays of anti-Blackness and oppression for what it is, call it out, and still perpetuate oppression and anti-Blackness in your practice through these smaller things we do too often go unexamined. We cannot give ourselves an out just because we can call out more blatant displays of oppression. Take, for example, Victoria's discussion of the shallow interpretations of hip-hop she saw. Like, that's oppressive! And I'm sure the teacher didn't think of it that way, you get what I'm saying?

Edmund Adjapong: I hear you 100%. Just demonstrating a level of awareness is not enough because Blackness is under attack. It's more so about what's the next step. We can demonstrate awareness and a level of humility around the work, but how do we get to the actionable steps, or what are we doing as individuals to counter anti-Blackness? It's difficult, but when we gather, when we organize, there's more of an opportunity to address the challenges and the blatant disregard for Black lives within schools.

Kelly Allen: Yeah, and I think what a lot of it comes down to is examining what your intent is in engaging with the work. Is your intent actually to center youth and co-create liberatory educational experiences with them, or is it to get them to sit down and be quiet so they can learn more to do better on these standardized tests? If your goal is just for students to sit down and be quiet and do better on standardized tests, you're still perpetuating oppression.

Edmund Adjapong: Yeah, it requires a reimagining of not only education systems, but also how we prepare our teachers to show up in these spaces.

So we had the opportunity to hear the freedom dreams of the folks that we had conversations with interviews with but what is your radical dream for the field of hip-hop and education?

Kelly Allen: You know, it's so wild that I have not even stopped to think about my freedom dream.

Edmund Adjapong: My freedom dream for the field of hip-hop and education has less to do with the actual field of hip-hop of education and more about like the context of education writ large, I think in this work and having these conversations, a theme that has come up a lot is educators abilities to engage in this work centered around youth culture or anything that may be distant from the norm. Ultimately, my freedom dream is for us to really make shifts and considerations around how we're training teachers and how we are utilizing culture within schools. When it comes to training teachers, obviously, teaching is very interpersonal. I dream that teachers will have the support and resources to engage in critical reflection about themself, their identities, about how they may or may not relate with their students. I believe that teachers will

	have less apprehension about leaning into leveraging youth culture, such as hip-hop within their working within their practice. You know, I see little to none of that within teacher education programs right now. Ultimately, I really love the process of learning. So take on this, this idea of leveraging their youth like youth culture in an authentic fashion, you know, they talked about that a lot. And, you know, I can recognize attempts that schools might make and that teachers might make, but I think there's an urgent need for us to push towards getting it right. Not just one space but across all spaces. Because we must find ways to counter the oppressive narratives and systems Black and brown communities are facing within the field of education.
Kelly Allen:	Yeah, I think ultimately, when I think about my freedom dream, it's bigger than hip-hop. I guess you could argue that every freedom dream is bigger than hip-hop, honestly. But, I think my freedom dream is that there will be a serious grappling with and eradication of anti-Blackness in our society, writ large. Not just in education, because education is just one institution in our community, and it is not like these anti-Black attitudes are only seen in education. These attitudes result from what people bring from other aspects of their lives. And so similar to you, I think that until we really grapple with the roots of anti-Blackness. It's kind of like, you know…I don't want to say, "What am I even doing?" But it's just always at the core of everything that I think about in this work. And it's hard because the racial realist in me sees how far we have to go as a society in understanding racism, and a part of that is recognizing that progress is slow and ongoing, and it's not necessarily something that I may ever see in my lifetime. But, my hope in continuing to work towards my freedom dream is that my children or my children's children may see progress in their lifetime. It's hard not to get too Afro-Pessimistic in the process, but the marathon continues.

Next Steps for Hip-Hop Educators

This book has been filled with the perspectives and freedom dreams of scholars and practitioners engaged in hip-hop education. While there were many varying perspectives demonstrated throughout this text, there were a few emerging themes that were consistent throughout including: educators must be willing to engage in critical introspective reflection, educators must center youth voices and perspectives and acknowledge how students engage with hip-hop culture, educators must be willing to allow students opportunities to lead and co-facilitate instruction, and educators must position themselves as lifelong learners. We want to conclude this book by offering some potential steps forward in this work.

1. **Be willing to engage in critical introspective reflection.**
   A prerequisite competency prior to any educator engaging in the praxis of hip-hop education is beginning the ongoing process of introspective reflection in regard to how their positionality in the world correlates or diverges from hip-hop culture. Educators must make sense of and navigate the tensions of what they enjoy, dislike, and appreciate and what aspects they prefer to highlight in regard to hip-hop culture. This critical introspective reflection will highlight some of our biases, which we all have, of hip-hop culture. For some, this critical introspective reflection will include an interrogation of whiteness and anti-Blackness. Once we understand our bias and the tensions we may have around some aspects of hip-hop culture, we can work toward making sense of them and ultimately eliminating them, which will allow for the authentic incorporation of hip-hop within our classroom spaces.

2. **Center youth voices and perspectives & acknowledging how students engage with hip-hop culture.**
   It's important to understand that individuals from different generations and geographical contexts may engage and appreciate hip-hop differently. Educators and researchers must set aside preconceived notions about how students engage with hip-hop culture to truly acknowledge and understand students' engagement with hip-hop culture. A key part of setting aside preconceived notions of students' engagement with hip-hop culture is questioning where these preconceived notions come from in the first place. Then, teachers and researchers must engage in intentional conversations with students about how they think about and engage with hip-hop. This new understanding of students' perspectives of hip-hop must be centered in the teaching and learning process. Centering youth voices and perspectives allows educators to gain an understanding of how their students' experience and engage in hip-hop culture. This understanding will be the foundation for how educators can leverage hip-hop within their classrooms.

3. **Allow students opportunities to lead and co-facilitate instruction.**
   Hip-Hop education is built on the premise that students' cultures should be centered. In order to center student culture within the

classroom, educators must create opportunities for students to lead and have actual ownership of the classroom space and instruction. Hip-Hop education counters oppressive concepts within education that position students as passive learners who must be molded into knowledgeable beings. Instead, hip-hop education positions students as individuals with incredibly rich experiential and cultural knowledge. Co-facilitation acknowledges that students are true experts in their cultures and encourages students to draw on the experiential and cultural knowledge they hold through the teaching and learning process. While engaging in the co-facilitation process can provide educators additional insight into how students engage and participate in hip-hop culture, ultimately, the goal of co-facilitation is for students to feel culturally acknowledged, respected, and affirmed.

4. **Educators must position themselves as lifelong learners.**
Lastly, there must be a recognition that culture is not static and is always evolving. As a result, educators must be dedicated to continuous learning, growth, and development as it relates to the culture of their students. Recognizing that culture is dynamic and fluid is necessary for positioning ourselves as lifelong learners. This is one reason educators must be malleable in thought and remain curious about the possibilities in relation to teaching and instruction.

We conceptualized this book as a space of radical possibility where we could freedom dream about the future of the field of hip-hop education. While this book does not claim to hold all of the answers, it is our hope that the conversations within this book are a step towards realizing liberatory educational practices through hip-hop.

Hip-Hop Education
Innovation, Inspiration, Elevation

Edmund Adjapong and Christopher Emdin, General Editors

Hip-Hop Education is a sociopolitical movement that utilizes both online and offline platforms to advance the utility of hip-hop as a theoretical framework and practical approach to teaching and learning. The movement is aimed at disrupting the oppressive structures of schools and schooling for marginalized youth through a reframing of hip-hop in the public sphere, and the advancement of the educative dimensions of the hip-hop culture. Hip-Hop Education's academic roots include, but are not limited to, the fields of education, sociology, anthropology, and cultural studies and it draws its most distinct connections to the field of hip-hop studies; which in many ways, is the stem from which this branch of study has grown and established itself.

The Hip-Hop Education: Innovation, Inspiration, Elevation series will be the first of its kind in educational praxis. It will be composed of books by artists, scholars, teachers, and community participants. The series will publish global authors who are experts in the fields of hip-hop, education, Black studies, Black popular culture, community studies, activism, music, and curriculum. Hip-Hop Education is explicit about its focus on the science and art of teaching and learning. This series argues that hip-hop embodies the awareness, creativity and innovation that are at the core of any true education. Furthermore, its work brings visibility to the powerful yet silenced narratives of achievement and academic ability among the hip-hop generation; reflecting the brilliance, resilience, ingenuity and intellectual ability of those who are embedded in hip-hop culture but also not necessarily academics in the conventional sense.

For additional information about this series or for the submission of manuscripts, please contact:

> editorial@peterlang.com

To order other books in this series, please contact our Customer Service Department:

> peterlang@presswarehouse.com (within the U.S.)

> orders@peterlang.com (outside the U.S.)

Or browse online by series:

> www.peterlang.com

www.ingramcontent.com/pod-product-compliance
Ingram Content Group UK Ltd.
Pitfield, Milton Keynes, MK11 3LW, UK
UKHW021326180426
11947UKWH00017B/1462